Readings and Feelings
An Introduction to Subjective Criticism

D1484412

Readings and Feelings
An Introduction to Subjective Criticism

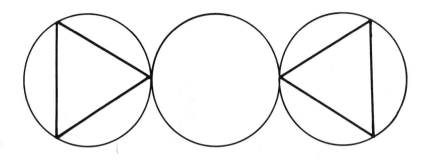

David Bleich
Indiana University

National Council of Teachers of English
1111 Kenyon Road, Urbana, Illinois 61801

NCTE Editorial Board: Richard Corbin, Charlotte S. Huck, Richard Lloyd-Jones, Roy C. O'Donnell, Owen Thomas, Robert F. Hogan, *ex officio*, Paul O'Dea, *ex officio.* Staff Editor: Duncan Streeter. Cover Design: Jean Fornango,

Library of Congress Catalog Card Number: 74-84482.
NCTE Stock Number: 39213.

Contents

Introduction

Almost all of us have spent a significant part of our childhood and youth in a classroom. Thinking back to this period in our lives yields a variety of interesting memories, some from in and around the classroom, and some having nothing to do with it. If we are honest with ourselves, I think we will have to admit that the interest of our school memories is patently emotional. Even if we recall those moments when we were conscious of having really learned something, we realize that the only reason we remember the experience is that it had some kind of emotional value for us. Perhaps it was a moment of real communication with a special teacher, or a whole year's relationship with a good teacher. Perhaps it was insight into our friends and enemies in school, the vivid memories of "catching on" to fractions or square roots, or the surprise of having actually enjoyed reading a book. Whatever we remember, whether it is the growth or the pain, it is the lingering emotion which gives those remembered scenes their vitality today.

Some of us have remained in school through adulthood and become teachers. In making the transformation to the other side of the desk, we have, presumably, been "educated" or enlightened as to what "really goes on in the classroom"—or should go on, perhaps. We are trained to enter the classroom with "ideas" and "methods" aimed at getting students to "understand" something. We are also trained to expect that only in rare instances will students come to "enjoy" what we are teaching and that we should remain content with being able to convey certain rudimentary skills necessary to handling our subject. It is not exactly that we are taught to place a low value on classroom enjoyment—rather, the opposite is the case: we are taught to *assume* that enjoyment can only come after understanding and skill-acquisition, that feeling in general can only be indulged in after the knowledge is acquired. The only feeling consciously confronted in the classroom is frustration, and then only because this feeling stands in the way of learning. The aim is less to understand this feeling than to conquer or eliminate it. The appearance of frustration in a student is not usually thought of as an occasion for insight but as a hurdle to be overcome. This basic separation of emotion from learning characterizes our overall attitude once we jump over to the other side of the desk.

This, by and large, however, is our conscious attitude rather than our more basic intuition. I doubt that any teacher will deny that confronting a class is an emotional situation, and that a magic tape-recording of his thoughts as he meets a class for the first time, for example, would certainly prove this to be the case. No matter how long we have been teaching, we continue to enter the classroom with feelings, with the physiological activity that normally accompanies feelings, and these feelings are governed by whatever mood we happen to be in that day. Of course, we make an immediate attempt to cast aside these conditions and proceed with the subject matter of the day. This shift is part of our trained conscious attitude that the student is there to get knowledge and the teacher is there to give it. The routine of class finds the teacher "correcting" the student, judging his performance, and quantifying its value in a grade. This larger classroom routine serves an important function: it averts the emotional demands of the classroom situation, it denies our uncertainties with regard to how to handle our feelings and those of our students, and it replaces our uncertainties with the simpler elements of exercising authority. If we abandon this routine, however, and allow ourselves to take more seriously our intuitions regarding the classroom situation—conceiving the class as a group of people with differing feelings, perceptions, and motives for being there to begin with—then we are forced to take into consideration how feelings and knowledge interact.

In recent years, the pressure to abandon some of the traditional formalities of the classroom has resulted in interesting new classroom activities, and at this time new ideas are legion. The call for "relevance," for example, is obviously an expression on the part of students and younger teachers of the need to *feel* the connection between knowledge and the overbearing emotional concerns of their lives. The need to feel the meaning of knowledge is not confined to active and restless minorities; it is present in all people to the degree that they wish to know anything at all. Certainly the biographies of those who achieved the most and the best in civilization show that not only does feeling precede knowledge but that knowledge is achieved only because of the *passion* to know and discover. The passion preceded the knowledge — not vice versa.

This is especially true with regard to knowledge about language and literature. Literature and art are perhaps the most directly human of the humanistic disciplines. The content of literature, its origin, and its effect on readers all call for sophisticated understanding of emotional life. The discipline of literary criticism is not simply the accumulation of knowledge about what was written, but the study of how, why, and what happens when *people* write and read. The history of criticism in modern times says that explication is the primary act of criticism. Critics must concentrate on "translating" literature into some other more intellectual language in order for the literature to be publicly received. This more or less "scientific" attitude has created the dangerous and false impression that a work of literature is objectively independent and that it somehow functions apart from those who write and read it. The fact is that a work of art or literature must be *rendered* so by a perceiver. If Max Brod did not read and publish Kafka's work, it would have no existence, even if it remained indefinitely in some vault. It is not just the "message" or the expressive essence of a work of literature that is created by the reader. The work itself would have no existence at all if it were not read. This is not simply a formulaic application of the old "if a tree falls in the forest . . ." paradox; with regard to symbolic works, *all* aspects of their existence, function, and effect depend on the processes by which they are assimilated by an observer. These processes are different in each individual, making the act of assimilation of special importance. To say that perceptual processes are different in each person is to say that reading is a wholly subjective process and that the nature of what is perceived is determined by the rules of the personality of the perceiver.

This book, therefore, aims to enlarge the normal purview of literary study to include the subjective bases and purposes for reading and coming to literary judgments. The overall aim is to provide a means for presenting literature in a way that will produce an internal motive for reading and thinking about literature. This motive is the awareness that reading can produce new understanding of oneself — not just a moral here and a message there, but a genuinely new conception of one's values and tastes as well

as one's prejudices and learning difficulties. In confronting literature from this point of view, we are not so much shifting the habits
of literary study as we are expanding them. Careful and precise
reading can never go out of style, and the techniques that have
accumulated toward this end remain as valid as they ever were.
But if careful and precise reading is the *only* thing stressed in
class, students and teachers alike easily lose sight of *why* one
should read carefully. Presented as it traditionally is, the main
reason for careful reading is moral—somehow it is unfair to the
text or to the author not to pay constant careful attention to it. Not
to read carefully represents defective discipline, or lack of respect,
or laziness, or sloppiness: it is some kind of personal misdemeanor
not to read carefully—and one gets lower grades for it. In place
of this moral and pedagogical authority brought to bear on any
alert student who asks, "Why should I read so carefully?" this
approach makes it possible to enlarge students' understanding of
their own behavior and thereby motivate them to read carefully
on their own, without external threat.

A major assumption of this technique is that all people, young
and old, think about themselves most of the time and think about
the world in terms of themselves. Biographies of important authors
have shown that even the greatest works of literature are most
comprehensively understood as expressions of the personalities
of the authors. Analogously, understanding and reconceptualizing
a work of literature can be best understood as expressions of the
personalities of the readers. The role of personality in response is
the most fundamental fact of criticism. Yes, there is an "object"
out there—a novel, a poem, a play—that has, seemingly, an objective existence, and one does need to be able to read to conceive of
it as an object. But just as one has to be motivated to learn to read,
one also has to be motivated to think about what one has read—or,
indeed, to take the initiative to read to begin with. Unless one has
had the experience of personal enlightenment from reading, one
is not aware that it is possible, and thus there is no way to become
motivated. The approach described in this book takes advantage
of a kind of "bank" of motives that all people have, motives derived from the instinctive concerns of being alive—pleasure,
self-esteem, intelligence, love. These motives can be attached
to any experience; that is, any experience that can be shown to
help a person fulfill these natural impulses will become an important experience to that person. I believe that reading and thinking
about literature can be made important to many in just this way.

As far as we now understand, personality is grounded in the
emotional history of an individual. For the first eighteen months

or so, a person's life is almost entirely physiological and emotional. Thought and knowledge do not begin until some time after that age. Thus the ongoing experience of peremptory feelings and images precedes the onset of deliberate thought. This basic developmental fact finds its aftermath in adult life in the peremptory nature of emotional experience, its automatic presence in our consciousness, a presence controlled only by deliberate mental activity on our part, and sometimes not even then. In daily life, any new perceptual experience stimulates an emotional response immediately, and our thought about this experience is a reaction to our emotional response plus the experience, rather than to the experience alone. It might seem, in order to justify this point of view, that a prolonged classroom presentation of personality theory is necessary. But this is not the case at all. Such a presentation, my experience has shown, has a deadening effect, except on the most enlightened and motivated students. Since our normal task is to stimulate motivation, not to rely on its presence beforehand, it is far more important to demonstrate the function of emotional response than to articulate it. Students can discover for themselves in their own lives the habits, the impulses, the feelings, and the imagery which form the basis of what we understand about personality development. Our initial and most important aim is to produce an *awareness* of one's own personality; the explanation of it comes later.

The course of study described in this book is divided into four phases, the length of each to last either a semester or a full year or more. The more time spent, the better, but the sequence is of primary importance. The first phase is "Thoughts and Feelings." The time is spent exploring the nature of feelings, how they appear, why, and how to distinguish between a feeling and a thought. The second phase is "Feelings about Literature." The normal capacity for emotional response is here studied in the particular context of a literary stimulus. The third phase is "Deciding on Literary Importance." This phase studies the relationship of intellectual judgment to emotional response. The fourth phase is "Interpretation as a Communal Act" and deals with the interest of others in one's own responses and interpretations. The logic of this sequence is that it proceeds outward, so to speak, from the most primitive, automatic, and unconscious experiences to the most complex and lately developed capacities—intellectual and communal thought and interaction. This technique may well be applicable to a number of other humanistic disciplines, but its application to literature is, I think, the most manifest, and for now, most fruitful.

While the poems that are discussed in the second section of this book are quoted in full, the stories and novels discussed in the last sections are not cited at all. They include D. H. Lawrence's "The Rocking-Horse Winner," Katherine Mansfield's "Her First Ball," Henry James's "The Turn of the Screw," and William M. Thackeray's *Vanity Fair*. Because these texts are available in a number of current anthologies, there is no need to reproduce them here. It is advisable, however, to read these works before reading the various responses to them, as well as my discussions of the responses.

Although it is not necessary to use the same works I have used in making my arguments, it might be of continuing interest to see how yet other students respond to these same works. It should be clear from the nature of my argument that while responses themselves will always vary, the mechanisms of emotional response will follow patterns similar to those found in the present responses to the above-mentioned works. Therefore, the teacher may choose his own texts according to principles consistent with his own style and tastes. Both the difficulty and the rewards of the method I am proposing lie in the variety of situations in which it may be applied, and in the variety of responses one will always get.

The method I am proposing is not simple and itself requires some study. It requires discipline on the part of both students and teacher, and I will indicate the various kinds as I proceed. But after six years of using this approach, I can say that it is really enjoyable and interesting for almost everyone. Above all, it produces the palpable feeling, surprising to most students, that reading a book or a poem can have some very important connections with the things that most concern and preoccupy them.

Thoughts and Feelings

As most of us are aware, students are trained, from the very first compositions in elementary school, to write down their thoughts and not their feelings. Almost every student from whom I have solicited written emotional responses reported that "I have never been asked to do anything like this in all my years at school." They also report being discouraged from using the pronoun "I" and from discussing personal impressions. Interpretive essays are encouraged to be as impersonal as possible, and in the university such essays are given the form of objective reporting. Part of the reason for this situation can be found in habits as old as civilization. Thought has always been considered to be manageable, social, disinterested, while feelings are unwieldy, private, and altogether preoccupied with the self. The traditional way to deal with feelings in group situations—but frequently in private as well—is to ignore or delay them, and follow one's rational thoughts as if they were utterly independent of how one feels.

First Impressions

Consider the elementary situation of walking into class, or if you are a student, of observing the teacher walk into class for the first time. There is little question that thought and judgment are going on in these early moments of a new class. If you are a student, you are in the process of "sizing up" the teacher and making judgments about him based on perceptual material which, if you stop to consider what it "proves," you easily realize proves nothing. Let us say you have a thought about the shabbiness of the teacher's suit, or more precisely, you make a mental note of this shabbiness. If you think about having made the note somewhat further, however, you realize that it is not the only thing you made a note of, that in fact you have assimilated an elaborate and detailed observation of the new teacher. Most importantly, each of these details that you remember noticing *already has a personal value attached to it*. That is, you have already made a decision as to the value of what you noticed. Indeed, the observation of a "shabby" suit is not simply an observation of *fact* but one of *value* as well. Now you might want to argue that all you noticed were facts about the new teacher, say, that he wore a green suit, was of medium height, was overweight, wore thick glasses, and did not look at the class too often until he began speaking. You may want to argue that these are only facts, but a moment's consideration here too reveals that there is a personal value in the use of words such as "medium," "overweight," and "thick." Someone shorter than the teacher would consider him "tall," someone fatter might think him "trim," and someone with thicker glasses would describe the teacher's as "ordinary." You may still want to argue that it is possible to make mental notes in even more precise terms, such as the exact height and weight of the teacher and the exact thickness of the glasses. Yes, it is possible to make such notes. However, in the situation we are discussing, it would be extremely rare for someone's first impressions to be phrased in those terms, but even if they were, ideas like "5-feet 7-inches, 165 pounds," and "¼-inch lenses" carry a value to the person making those estimates, and the actual numerical presentation of these observations represents the individual's personal style of delivering these impressions rather than a statement of fact. The truth is that this particular observer did not measure the teacher or his glasses, and the numbers serve only as connotative descriptions, not denotative facts. Altogether, one cannot escape assigning value to the automatic impressions one gets; moreover, this value is always present, whether implicitly or explicitly, in the words used to articulate one's impressions.

Let us examine a smaller-scale, more detailed instance of how feelings operate on early perceptual experience. Suppose you are talking with a friend and you meet a new person whose nose makes a strong impression on you. Afterward, you remark to your friend, "What a finely shaped nose he has." In terms of the habits of ordinary discourse, you are offering your companion what you think is a fact that you observed and are implicitly asking if he too observed the same fact. What produced this observation, however, was not a mechanical process of recording the nose in imagery and then translating the image into spoken words. If this were the case, everyone who noticed the nose would come out with precisely the same thoughts and even the same words. On the contrary, your observation of the nose was immediately subject to a series of decisions and internal mental events which ultimately produced the observation to your friend. The important event in this series is your emotional response, not articulated in words but amounting to something like, "I like that nose," and you have no direct consciousness of its specific shape, even though that shape was part of your perception. Now there is another mental event—the desire to present your impression to your friend. This desire initiates a swift review of your perception to bring it more fully into consciousness, and then you advance the thought to your friend. The important event in your rearticulation of the thought is your translation of it from a subjective mood to the objective. The *subject* of your private thought was *you*, naturally, and the *subject* of the public thought was *nose*. In presenting your private feeling, you *objectified* it, subtly shifting the emphasis from yourself to something outside yourself. Your objective statement, however, includes the value you attach to your perception, the value showing up in the word "finely." In the process of attaching the value, *you suppress your active role in creating it* to begin with. Therefore, it is not simply a matter of habit and tradition to avoid speaking of one's own feelings; our linguistic forms for discourse seem especially to facilitate speaking of what we perceive to be outside ourselves before speaking of what we know to be inside. And psychologically it is safer to speak of something other than ourselves, even though what is most important is the test of our own judgment that such a statement represents.

Getting an Emotional Response in Class

Our aim in this part of the unit is to learn to disclose the series of subjective events which always precedes the announcement of a judgment and to demonstrate their causal relationship with this judgment. While it is possible in class to use the kind of material I have just offered by, say, asking the class to report what their feelings were when the teacher first walked into class, it is easier and more convincing to provoke the class into an emotional response. Most students are fairly shy at first. A class may be significantly provoked in a relatively safe way by writing an inflammatory proposition on the board. One of my favorites is a statement like, "Men are smarter than women," or, if you prefer,

"Women are smarter than men." Or writing a mild smutty term like "son of a bitch!" in big letters. These have never failed to elicit responses strong enough to create a prolonged discussion.

Consider the first statement. Responses range from an immediate "yucchhh!" to "I don't think that's true." There is also laughter, and every now and then someone calls out "bullshit!" Few people will come right out and agree with the statement, but those who laughed probably believe it is at least partly true and want to keep this fact a secret. Others will have laughed because they immediately perceived that they were being deliberately provoked. Those who offered a vigorous negative response may not have liked being provoked, may also have considered the thought outrageous regardless, or both. It is not easy to distinguish immediately the exact causes of these responses, but it is very easy to indicate that there was an instantaneous feeling evoked that is not easily distinguished from the respondent's intellectual opinion.

The main question to organize the subsequent discussion around is, What is it you think you are reacting to? It is necessary to try to understand each of the different responses and what they mean. The first step is to try to enlarge the various responses by asking the respondents to elaborate, if they would, on their feelings, and to remember what each of, say, five people said. Here the *styles* of responses of the different respondents are extremely relevant, and an analysis of these styles promises to tell us something new about the individual's ideas and tastes that he probably did not already know.

There will always be a direct correspondence between the nature of the response and the manner in which it is offered. In some of the more emphatic responses, the respondents did not formulate their thoughts and instead chose the quickest and most emphatic way to express their feelings. A more thoughtful response could be construed as an instantaneous response, but here other matters enter into the consideration, such as the tone in which it is rendered, or whether the respondent raised his hand rather than calling out. The latter is true of all the "gut" reactions: no student will raise his hand and then say "yucchhh." It is important to call attention to this explanatory feature of the response because rarely in any class are particular manners scrutinized by the teacher as a means of understanding response and/or judgment. "Bad" manners are usually dealt with by admonitory authority, or if they are overlooked, they are also not analyzed; they are automatically considered to be irrelevant to the "content" of what is under discussion.

There is no way to tell whether the quick reactors will be more willing to discuss their responses than the slower ones. Hopefully both will be willing to investigate their reactions, and I will here proceed on that assumption. In any case, the process of trying to understand each style is the same—an informal classroom interview, with the rest of the class participating if they wish.

Guidelines for Obtaining Emotional Response

The guidelines for such interviews are a fundamental part of the method of subjective criticism and will be used in more elaborate form when the class ultimately moves on to literature and critical judgments. Furthermore, it takes some practice to acquire a feel for these guidelines, and they cannot really be used until the teacher develops an internal intuitive sense regarding their ultimate function and usefulness. There are two basic components which contribute to any individual's emotional response to anything—*affect* and *association*.

Affect

Affect is a kind of raw emotion and is usually describable in very familiar terms—anger, love, jealousy, indignation, contentment, and so on. Such feelings are usually accompanied by physiological correlatives—changes in heartrate, perspiration, respiration, and the like—and they are easy to spot for that reason. Affect is also what most people are most likely to tell you about when you ask them how they are feeling about something. Affect is usually easy to notice and easy to communicate—provided one is willing in the first place, of course. There is also an inward, subjective advantage to reporting an affect: it tends to resist explaining in terms that are any more specific, while giving the impression of forthrightness and candor. Therefore, it is to be expected that if an individual is willing to tell his feelings at all in the first place, one should expect an affective report, followed by a desire to terminate the interview, though, of course, this latter desire need not occur.

In the particular example I offered—men are smarter than women—the gut reactors will announce their outrage; they will accuse the teacher of "male chauvinism," perhaps of sadism. Perhaps there will be perorations regarding the ongoing social injustice, how it is about time this sort of thing should stop, how it is not funny even as a joke. All of the "arguments," we should note, while obviously admissible on an independent basis, are here used as justifications for the initial outrage, perhaps as a way of excusing the bad manners or the sudden display of emotion.

Regardless of their validity, that is their function for the outraged individual. From the standpoint of our study of the response, the ensuing arguments simply underscore and make more explicit the quality and strength of the original affect. They do relatively little to explain why a particular person felt a particular affect in response to this statement. The more thoughtful respondents would probably advance the very same arguments, though probably in a different tone of voice, and express their emotion or affect as something like disappointment, surprise, or anxiety that a teacher should raise such a thought for consideration. In this case too, the arguments do very little to really get to the personal roots of the first reaction.

Association

To get to the roots of these first reactions, associative analogies are necessary. Collecting such analogies is similar to the original psychoanalytic technique of understanding an individual through free association. This method works by asking the individual to relax his mind, reimagine the stimulus, observe what appears in his mind spontaneously, and report these thoughts without prior censorship. It is not hard to see that this is a difficult process and that, especially in a new class, there is every reason to suppose that it would not succeed very well. After all, what student in a room full of people he has never met before would relax his mind and speak out whatever comes into it? While such reluctance exists, it remains no obstacle since, in the early phases of class, the full, elaborate process of free association is not necessary or desirable. What is needed is for one of the respondents to let his mind wander for a rather brief time and to report perhaps one or two analogies for the affect he has reported. One can even coax this student, through explanation, for such analogies, i.e., ask him what kinds of events in his life provoked the same feelings. It is an answerable question for almost anyone, and it usually produces relevant and discussable material. All the respondent has to do is remember an anecdote whose common link with the present is the similarity of affect. The question now arises as to how one evaluates and makes use of this anecdotal material.

Making Use of Anecdotal Material

First, a warning. To some there might be the temptation to perform a quick Freudian analysis of the association and to apply the meaning thus derived as the explanation of the affect in question. That would be a dangerous and irresponsible course.

In no instance is one ever analyzing a person. I find this warning necessary because on each occasion that I introduce the method, a zealous student catches on to it quickly and immediately makes a clinical diagnosis of the respondent. This is precisely what should *not* happen, and it constitutes the greatest danger of this method. No respondent is a patient and no disease is being sought. The analysis of a response is an attempt to reach understanding and not an attempt to cope with illness or change behavior. Any diagnosis performed in class by either student or teacher will destroy the sense of mutual trust and common search for understanding. It is necessary to stress this point repeatedly in the opening meetings of a class using this method. Indeed, it is worth spending two or three days making the distinction between the analysis of a response and the analysis of a person. However, once this is done, the class is almost always reassured and work can proceed.

Traditionally, in the therapeutic process, there are no hard and fast rules regarding "good" or "bad" associations, and, in principle, everything can actually be put to some use because the patient lets it come to mind. While this principle remains true, it is equally true that certain materials of free association are produced for purposes of obstructing further inquiry, while other materials palpably facilitate the process of self-understanding. Additionally, the many years of experience with the method of free association have shown what kinds of material in a person's life history are most psychologically germane. There is an increasing faith, most notably demonstrated in the works of Erik Erikson and other important biographers like Leon Edel, that the systematic character of each personality can be determined by the history of his relationships with others. Almost all neurotic problems are characterized by a disturbance of the ability to conduct satisfactory relationships. The key sign that any given association retains a significant leverage for someone is the extent to which it involves an important relationship in his life. If the association is important yet does not manifestly bespeak such a relationship, it is likely that its real importance derives from its intimate association with a relationship which is as yet unspoken. Psychology has shown that a person responds first and most to the sensations and demands of his own body, then of his own person, and then of the people about him. Experience not connected with any of these areas enters consciousness as a subordinate function of these three areas and develops value only in this subordinate function. While one cannot claim to be able to find definite proof of this proposition, my experience has been that this principle of understanding associative material has yielded considerable enlightenment in class.

When associative analogies are presented in class, therefore, one can decide on their authenticity rather soon by simply noting how important a relationship is used to demonstrate the affect under scrutiny. I might add, however, that in these opening "demonstration" sessions one need not look too closely, and one can rely as well on whether the association feels authentic to the listener. In the beginning one may use this principle just as a way of deciding which among a number of associative analogies one will choose to discuss at greater length.

The understanding of the association depends a great deal on the context in which it is solicited. In this particular case, as I had suggested earlier, there is some question as to whether the response is to the statement itself or to the fact that a certain person wrote that certain statement on the board at that moment. If we follow our rule of thumb, it is safe to assume that the response is caused by the individual's perception of what the statement represents about the person making it. That is, the respondent with the strong negative reaction is offended by a *person*, the teacher, from whom he expected a great deal. The response as a whole—affect plus association—represents a feeling about a newly defined and relatively important relationship. Therefore, if the teacher is a man and the respondent a woman, the outrage and the association defining it are easily connected with the content of the actual statement: the respondent correctly concludes that she has been "attacked," however symbolically, however deliberately or facetiously, by the teacher. Respondents who "see" the tongue-in-cheek quality of the offense will nevertheless feel the offense, but will express this offense in a more understanding form—laughter. They will laugh at having been "had," and will thereby express their understanding of the unreal quality of the offense.

This latter understanding is not necessarily "truer" than the understanding of the more seriously offended respondent. For our purposes, the objective truth is not the real question. Our only aim has been to demonstrate the process by which two different people arrive at two different responses and to show two different ways of responding to their own responses. The third respondent, who neither laughed nor was offended and said simply "I don't think that is true," shows yet another personal style. This respondent perhaps felt the offense, but controlled whatever feelings he or she may have had, and then objectified these feelings, awaiting further discussion to resolve them. In traditional classrooms, this latter attitude would be considered the best—the most mature, the most acceptable, and the most desirable—and all other students would be invited to emulate it. Now there is no question that this is a fine attitude or personal style. But the other attitudes, which proceed more directly from the personal feelings involved in response, reveal just as much and perhaps even more of the class's subjective experience in responding to a particular stimulus. When the associations of all three respondents are ultimately bared, it will become clear indeed that each individual is just as complex as the other. Each can well have achieved important insight into himself and his style of response as well as into his attitudes about the teacher and the proposition on the blackboard.

The associations are the key to this insight. They represent a sample of what aspect of the personality was engaged in this experience—and that is all that they represent. They cannot be taken as important evidence of a person's covert subscription to doctrines of male chauvinism or feminine inferiority, or worse, as evidence of self-hatred, and so on. These are diagnoses which have no place in the classroom, and their truth or falsehood is irrelevant to the work of self-enlightenment in the classroom context. It is up to the individual student to record his own various responses and to assess his tastes as they develop in the course. If he would like professional help in analyzing these tastes as a function of his whole personality, he can certainly get such help. The aim in class is to understand how people respond emotionally and then translate these responses into thoughts and judgments.

The Role of the Teacher

It should be clear from my discussion regarding the collection and use of associative responses that this is not a gut-spilling operation or a "touchy-feely" group experience. All feelings and responses are not equally valuable or equally honest or equally consequential. Some people don't wish to offer honest or consequential responses and are afraid to say so. They will consciously offer trivial responses just to avoid being conspicuous. Others will offer nothing until they are more sure of what is going on. Still others will blurt out anything that comes into their minds, conceiving of this situation as the long-awaited opportunity to tell the world how important they are. And finally, many will be glad of the chance to look into their feelings and study them respectfully and seriously. The discipline involved here is not merely one of finding real affective responses and psychologically germane associations; it further obliges the teacher to pay attention to which students offered which feelings and associations and to keep them straight in his mind. This is not easy and takes effort, patience, and experience.

There is yet a more important discipline incumbent upon the teacher—that is, he must realize that he is subject to these same rules of response. He must be ready to offer samples of his own responses and to explain his own feelings and thoughts in ways no different from what he expects from his students. This is probably the most important thing he can do to establish an atmosphere of trust and honesty and yet still maintain the necessary distance between individuals. No matter how the seating arrangements in class are turned around, no matter whether first names or last names are used, no matter whether the teacher wears suits or jeans, the teacher has the authority in the class, and the class will not function unless this authority is exercised in a productive way. The teacher is older, as a rule, and more experienced in just being alive. But even if he is not older, he has the authority of training and prolonged thought about what he is doing in class, and students, no matter how old, simply have not thought as long and as carefully about the subject as the teacher has. If this is not the case, the teacher should not yet be in the classroom.

In this method, leadership is best exercised through example. Most students in high school and college want and need to emulate older people. They are in the process of trying to find out who they are, what they like and what they don't. They are intensely preoccupied with themselves, and in spite of many appearances to the contrary, are instinctively looking for ways to make a subject part of themselves either as a solution to, or an escape from, their preoccupations. If the teacher can quickly and clearly convey the fact that he is aware of these needs, that he has had them too, and that he is there to help them with these concerns, he will greatly facilitate the process of emulation. The student will be able to make good use of his natural desire to identify with and adopt—and adapt—the thought processes of the teacher. Even if a good student seems independent or contrary or rebellious, it is a good bet that these manifestations represent a response to the teacher—that is, the student has a strong need to change what is being taught before making it his own. It is likely, for example, that those who make a strong show of rejecting the suggestion to look closely at their feelings nevertheless want to do so, but they find it difficult to "go along" for other subjective reasons. While these reasons cannot be probed directly in class, it is worthwhile spending as much time as possible publicly discussing these students' opinions and feelings about the issue. My experience has been, however, that there is no student who does not wish to understand his feelings better and to make use of this understanding in his schoolwork.

A silent rule in this technique that does not obtain in the traditional classroom is that one makes *conscious use* of an adolescent student's preoccupation with himself. This rule has a specific consequence, and this consequence was implicit in the selection of a "provocative" or "inflammatory" statement. Whether or not traditional authorities care to admit it, sexuality is the cardinal concern of adolescents. It is of concern less as a subject matter than as an overbearing fact of development—physiological, psychological, and social. Issues of politics and religion are also provocative, but the bodily and psychological bases of such issues are much weaker than those of sexuality. It has appeared to certain critics of this technique that the use of sexuality is an assault by the teacher in the service of voyeuristic impulses. This may happen, but it obviously need not be the case, especially with an enlightened teacher who has learned to manage his own sexuality. There is, furthermore, a principle operating that serves to prevent such degeneration, namely, that teachers have also gone through adolescence, that teachers have struggled with fantasies, impulses, and curiosities just as students do now. This common participation in the developmental process will easily render the topic of sexuality a powerful one. This approach will fail only if the teacher is not ready to admit to himself and to his class that he has that much in common with his class. If he does not admit this, he cannot share his responses with his class, and if he does not share his responses, he cannot use this technique.

I may now point out how this silent rule—that one make conscious use of adolescents' preoccupations—operated in all of the examples I have used to demonstrate the presence of emotional response. There were three instances—observing a new teacher for the first time, remarking about someone's nose, and provoking response by saying that "men are smarter than women." None of these instances are sexual in the usual sense, but they relate to perceptual habits and thoughts that are directly concerned with most adolescents' personal preoccupations. First, observing someone's body, and making a judgment about its size and appearance. It is familiar how adolescents spend important time in front of the mirror estimating their potential as a visual attraction. The observation of others with these concerns in mind is therefore one more occasion to exercise a habit which is already well established as a function of the student's stage of development. Then, observing a nose, and deciding whether one likes it or not. Of course, one can immediately get some sensational Freudian mileage from "nose" jokes, but regardless of how many jokes are made, the concern with *particular parts* of one's body—muscles, breasts, hair, and so on—is notoriously great among adolescents. And how many adolescents have rhinoplasty performed? Even though the outward context of this example is apparently bland, its associative potential is extremely great. Finally, my seemingly invidious comparison of women to men. This may be seen to touch upon many things, but any juxtaposition of men and women with a view toward exposing the differences has an important stimulative effect on adolescents—and probably on most adults as well. The sense of the difference between the sexes is itself different in all people and is therefore an especially likely way to demonstrate differences in personality style. Then there is the nonsexual question of "smartness." By seeming to relate this nonsexual question with the sexual one, the statement constitutes an offense to common patterns of thought. But it is a special kind of nonsexual issue. Try saying that "men are richer than women" and compare the intensity of response. Smartness is a psychological issue, just as sexuality is, and it is frequently viewed in our culture as a mental form of sexuality. The covert psychological issue that this statement plays upon is, "how sexual a person am I," which is one of the most fundamental concerns of the adolescent mind. One might argue with cogency that money is an economic form of sexuality, but somehow money does not touch the same responsive chords in most people that the special combination of smartness and sexuality does. Knowledge, and the ability to get it, is a concern of all people since childhood, in all cultures. But money is never a spontaneous childhood concern and therefore exercises its fascination on most adults only insofar as it stands for other, more fundamental psychological needs or wishes. And finally, the question of smartness and knowledge calls attention to the ongoing activity in the classroom.

One may have other objections to my particular examples. I could certainly explain why my personality chose the particular examples it did, even though my glasses are not ¼-inch thick. My aim has been to articulate the principles which guide one's choice of examples for eliciting concerned emotional response from the class, the discussion of which examples would be enlightening and would bring a few good chuckles. This principle is that an adolescent student—ages 12 to 22—is intensely preoccupied with his own person—physically, psychologically, and socially. He shares in common with people of all ages a fundamental concern about the relationships and people in his life. These preoccupations and concerns are the key to bringing out a new, serious awareness and understanding of the role of emotional life in intellectual development.

Feelings about Literature

Introduction: The Subjective Orientation

Once a person has seen his responses in action in a general way and how they are constantly functioning, literature becomes less a subject he learns in school than a special opportunity to engage the emotions and thoughts foremost in his mind. Most people believe they know exactly what literature is; they believe they can recognize it when they see it even if they can't articulate a "definition." One of the results of exploring the feelings that arise in response to a single sentence written on the blackboard is that the assumed sense of what constitutes literature is called into question. The "itness" or objectivity of the actual phrase on the board loses its force. Norman Holland, in *The Dynamics of Literary Response,* performs a small experiment in order to demonstrate what is meant by "the willing suspension of disbelief." He quotes a prose passage that could pass for either history or literature and then asks his reader to examine the difference between what went on in his mind when he thought it was history versus what went on when he thought it was literature. Holland does not explore anyone's actual response, but he does report that he himself feels much more relaxed mentally when he reads the passage as literature. His conclusion is that "it is the expectation we bring to the paragraph that determines the degree to which . . . we test it for the truth." While Holland's distinction between the search for truth and the search for relaxed pleasure is important, another finding, implicit in his experiment, is of particular interest to our discussion. That is, *it is the reader*

who determines whether a piece of writing is literature. Sometimes, in practice, this mental act is not necessary because we
believe it when we are told that a certain work is literature.
But this only means that someone else decided it was literature,
and we, by our own mental act, agreed that the previous act
will also be our own. Our point is that a piece of writing *becomes*
literature as a result of a subjective decision that it is literature.
If you suspect that this may be a tautological point, just think
of the Bible. Some read this book as if it were literature, some as
if it were history, and some as if it were God's word. The only
thing that all readers can agree on about the Bible is that it is a
book. Obviously this is a rather trivial agreement, and the question
of what the book is "essentially" is altogether determined by the
individuals and groups of individuals who read the book and
react to it.

To be sure, one does not spend much time thinking about
whether a poem is a poem. The relevance of our private decision
that it is a poem is that we are once again reminded that the
essence of a symbolic work is not in its visible sensory structure
or in its manifest semantic load but in its subjective re-creation
by a reader and in his public presentation of that re-creation.
We will explore this re-creation by dividing it into three phases—
perception, affective response, and associative response.

Perceiving the Work

In examining different modes of perception we will study an
exercise frequently performed in introductory literature classes.
We will study the work of seven students of a class that was asked
to "say what the poem says" in their own prose. As a rule, exercises such as this, as well as the kind of investigations carried
out by I. A. Richards in *Practical Criticism,* aim to point out
mistakes in reading. This, of course, will not be our goal. Our aim,
rather, will be to try to understand the patterns of perceptual
emphasis in each reader and to suggest how these patterns will
be relevant in understanding the reader's larger patterns of
response and judgment. There are some who will say that retelling
a poem in any other words but its own does some kind of violence
to the poem. However, since we do not assume the inviolability
of a poem beyond maintenance of the text, and since we further
believe that the simple act of reading produces a subjective
change in the text, we may reasonably assume that the prose
presentation of a poem represents the reader's subjective perception of it.

A Drumlin Woodchuck

One thing has a shelving bank,
Another a rotting plank,
To give it cozier skies
And make up for its lack of size.

My own strategic retreat
Is where two rocks almost meet,
And still more secure and snug,
A two-door burrow I dug.

With those in mind at my back
I can sit forth exposed to attack
As one who shrewdly pretends
That he and the world are friends.

All we who prefer to live
Have a little whistle we give,
And flash, at the least alarm
We dive down under the farm.

We allow some time for guile
And don't come out for a while
Either to eat or drink.
We take occasion to think.

And if after the hunt goes past
And the double-barreled blast
(Like war and pestilence
And the loss of common sense),

If I can with confidence say
That still for another day,
Or even another year,
I will be there for you, my dear,

It will be because, though small
As measured against the All,
I have been so instinctively thorough
About my crevice and burrow.

Consider the following restatements of the poem.

A.   In order to feel secure, many animals find themselves a hiding place. Some choose a shelflike river bank, while others choose a piece of rotting timber. My own retreat is a burrow between two rocks which almost touch one another. I dug the burrow myself and made two entrances to it. I always know that there is a safe place just behind me, so I can sit out in the open and pretend as if I'm not afraid of anything. But when any of us hear the danger signal from the other animals, we each scurry to our own hiding places. Then we sit and wait, thinking about the games of life and death until the hunters pass by. I think of my shelter and my safety from day to day, and year to year, and I know that the tiny little hole that I have made so naturally is the only reason that I go on living.

B. Small animals are constantly in danger; we depend on our instinct to keep alive. One safety measure is our homes—our nests or burrows. Some of us find niches and crannies in banks of earth, others build on rotten boards or other debris left by man. Since we're too small to stand up and fight man face to face, and our legs are too short to get away from dogs, we must hide to protect ourselves. We rely on our burrows for safety. We tunnel into the earth. Here, surrounded by the ground on all sides, we feel at home and safe.

For my own home, I chose a special spot. It is easily accessible in case of danger, yet hidden from normal view. Only I know that the two rocks that almost touch mark the path to my burrow. Besides being well hidden, my burrow itself goes far into the ground. The intricate tunnels keep me close and safe. If a dog does smell me out and finds my hole, and even if he's small enough to fit down, I can still escape—I've dug a secret rear exit for just such emergencies.

Knowing I've planned well and my burrow is a good retreat, I can go about my business in full view. I can pretend to be careless and nonchalant. But if danger is really imminent, the others and I have a signal—we give a shrill whistle as soon as any of us senses danger. When the warning sounds, we dive for our burrows—and safety. We do not come out—not for food or water or anything—until we are positive all danger is passed. Wisely, we wait.

And if after the dogs and hunters and noise of guns and whine of bullets have all died out, if I am again passed over and left alive, it is because (although I'm a small and insignificant creature of God's world) I planned my hideaway carefully and I am prepared for trouble.

C. Everything on earth has some means, no matter how crude, of securing its comfort and protection. As for myself, I have cleverly devised a twofold plan of protection. My little retreat, in the first place, is well hidden by its natural surroundings; secondly, I have two entrances to the place, making an escape quite easy if necessary.

With the knowledge that I am secure against any danger presented by the world, I can appear to be brave by exposing myself to almost any danger. I know I am well protected, but other people don't and think me quite courageous.

Let me tell you about my strategy—mine and my friends who choose to live as I do. If any one of us detects danger, he warns the rest of us. We then retreat from the outside world and the danger, remaining secure and comfortable in our various burrows. We are smart enough to remain withdrawn until the danger is completely gone. We're really very clever about the whole thing.

Yet, when the danger passes, whatever it may have been—natural or manmade—if I am well and can hope to live a little longer, I owe it to one thing: my shrewdness. You see, I may be small in comparison with the rest of the world, but it's not my physical size that counts. Instead, it's my mental size, my capacity to be clever in living my life, that really adds up to something.

For accuracy, these are all rather good restatements. They speak in the speaker's voice and they cover a significant part of the factual material in the original. If we so desired, we could say fairly easily that these three respondents perceived the poem "correctly." As we will see, however, this is not altogether true, and the mistakes and distortions in each restatement add up to a personal expression of style.

Response A is relatively spare and concentrates on the speaker's logic. Almost all of the particulars in the poem are omitted—the rotting plank, the farm, war and pestilence, the whistle, for example. More importantly, however, almost all of the important feelings are also omitted—coziness, security, confidence, shrewdness, alarm. The poem is restated as if it were a report. There is an emphasis on what the speaker knows about himself and his burrow. Such omissions do not necessarily represent inaccuracies of perception. On the contrary, they represent the perception of a particular train of thought—"this is a poem about the speaker's quiet understanding of how to remain safe and live long"—something *we have also seen* in the poem. For this reason, the restatement seems accurate. Even the brevity of the restatement should be taken as a representation of the brevity and concision of thought this respondent gets from the poem. We may say that this particular reader was disposed to selecting this logical, concise element in the poem as representing his own response. There does remain one further important omission in this restatement, made by the other two in this series as well, but we will return to it subsequently.

Response B differs significantly from A not simply in its more discursive presentation, but also in the fact that it inserts details that are not literally to be found in the poem. Such a restatement may seem more obviously revealing of subjective perception, but it is not in fact either more or less subjective. This respondent suggests a particular fear—of dogs—that is not found in the poem. Further, B explains that the speaker's fear of dogs comes from the fact that he thinks his legs are too short to escape from them. The dogs even may smell the speaker out of his hole, and they are accompanying a hunting party which poses the overall threat. B inserts other interesting details—she explains the burrows as another kind of nest; she says that some of the animals find "niches" in the banks of the earth and that homes are sometimes made in "other debris left by man." She then inserts the explicit fear of "fight[ing] man face to face," and adds that the safety of the burrow derives from its being "surrounded by ground on all sides." Then, the "almost touch[ing]" rocks "mark the path" to the burrow—which they do not do in the poem. The whole presentation of the dog smelling out the speaker is embellished by the thought that the dog may even be small enough to fit down the hole. Finally, the poem's "little whistle" is converted by B into a "shrill whistle." Our question is, Is there any pattern in these interesting additions to the poem? I think we may say that respondent B enlarged the poem in ways analogous to how respondent A narrowed its focus. B made the poem into a *more* dramatic experience. The speaker here is more conscious of his own weakness, of the fact that the threats are coming from particular sources of great strength. Man is in the picture prominently—accordingly, the need for safety is greater—"surrounded by ground on all sides." For the same reason, the little whistle becomes "shrill." Altogether, B "sees" the perilous elements in the story much more prominently than A and senses a more immediate, more precarious situation being recounted by the speaker. The added details, therefore, cannot be seen as "errors." They express an element in the poem on which I think many would agree: a sense in which the speaker is not all that logical and calm and is in fact involved in a rather important and crucial drama.

In contrast, C emphasizes the speaker's self-satisfaction with regard to his cleverness and employs a different set of insertions and exaggerations. We should immediately note that the word "clever" does not appear in this poem, even though it becomes an important element in C's restatement. The poem does mention shrewdness, guile, and confidence, but even so the emphasis placed by C on cleverness is an exaggeration. For example, C translates "my own strategic retreat" as "I have cleverly devised," thus inserting the element of self-congratulation where the original was less personal. In her second paragraph C attributes to the speaker a thought about "other people," which also does not appear explicitly in the poem. C transfers the term "strategy" to the account of the contingency plan and then translates, "we allow some time for guile" (this refers presumably to expected deceit on the part of the threatening agency) as "we are smart enough to remain withdrawn." That is, the smartness mentioned in the poem is transferred to the speaker, and then C adds the additional superfluous comment, "We're really very clever about the whole thing." Finally, in her last paragraph, the speaker's profession of confidence and of instinctive thoroughness is translated as "my shrewdness," "my mental size," and "my capacity to be clever." Here again, the respondent transfers a word used earlier in the poem to a situation she later sees. This transference demonstrates how we allow a poem to create a mood in us: we automatically apply earlier images we had to later situations.

C's stress on mental capacity resembles A's restatement in that the stress is on the control or the victory of the speaker. The causes of the particular form these emphases take are personal. However, not only the exaggerations or additions are rooted in personal factors. The entire perception of the poem is so rooted, where the exaggerations serve as signals of these roots. There can be any number of reasons why these respondents picked out the things they did, but one of these reasons may be that none of the three cared to include in their perception a reference to the line, "I will be there for you, my dear," which suggests that the whole poem is an address to someone "dear" to the speaker, perhaps a lover. This is precisely the way two other respondents perceived this poem—completely informed by this one line:

D. Hello Dear,

As you probably know in this place of unrest, most of us need some sort of shelter of one kind or another to make our world a little more secure. It is a necessary precaution which the foolish ones refuse to realize to make up for our small stature. Several of my neighbors provided themselves with old rotten boards; a couple of others decided on the bank.

However, I wish you could see my place that I finally found. I don't think anything else could beat it.   It is isolated in the woods between two rocks. For days, I have been working carving an entrance and an exit. I cannot tell you what a difference it makes just knowing that it is there. Sometimes when I get bored, I play this game. I sit on the outside, pretending I do not know that the hunter is there until the last second. I try to look very nonchalant like I am somehow above it all. I assume the air that everything is best in the best of all possible worlds. Yet, I cannot wait too long. I sure would hate to be a dead woodchuck. When I get too scared I whistle to calm myself, then I dash into my shelter. Since it is not easy to tell if I am still being hunted, I stay there for quite a long time devoting my time to contemplating the issues of the day.

I especially try to figure out why the hunter with the double-barreled shotgun is so quick to kill. I can never come up with any other solution than that he is evil, like war, disease, and madness.

All my confidence against danger rests in my burrow. If I keep alive from day to day or year to year, it is because I have equipped myself well. Now neither food nor drink seems to me more important.

A refuge is the most important thing in the world, it is the only defense against humans that I know.

Well, remember I will always be here waiting for you.

Love, Me

E.   God! You know, sometimes I get so fed up with people and the way they act and with the world and all its troubles that I just want to get away from it all. Kind of crawl into a hole like a groundhog does. I suppose a nice sloping hill I could hide behind or an old, rotted plank I could sort of crouch on would serve my purpose. But a hole's a little more secure, more snug somehow.

I don't know exactly what I'd do with my hole. I guess just sit around and wait till some unpleasant, personal something-or-other happened. Then I'd kind of jump into the hole head first and just sit. At first I'd think about apple pie or my first really nice kiss or some other nice-to-think-about thing. But I'd probably wind up thinking about what had driven me into my hole this time. I'd plan cunning deeds of how I could get back at my oppressors.

And then, after my moment of treacherous thoughts had passed, after I'd regained my common sense (the loss of which I would dutifully blame on the outside world, of course), I'd try to go back to pleasant thoughts. And if I could do this, these thoughts would no longer be of pies and kisses, but they'd be thoughts of YOU, my dear.

I feel that if time and time again I can emerge from my hole a sound and whole member of this human race, this vast universe, and be there for YOU, if I can do this much, it is only because I have been so instinctively thorough about my crevice and burrow.

D's conception of the poem as a love note includes so many extra details that it does not pay to point them out individually. The overall sense of the note is the consciousness of intimate conversation, which D inserts *before* the actual text of the transcription, although in the poem one does not become aware of this intimacy until the end. For the first three respondents this end-placement seemed to diminish its importance, whereas D and E take the line as a defining characteristic. This demonstrates the sense in which the perception of the poem is a subjective reconstruction rather than a simple recording of facts. D also must have responded with a feeling of love, since that is what she makes explicit, in the final signature. Pursuant to this conception, D views the material of the poem almost as an invitation by the speaker to his beloved to join him in "my place that I finally found," while we observe that in the poem, the speaker makes no reference to having searched for and "finally found" the right place. While the dominant theme of personal security is retained in the note, it is portrayed on the one hand as "the only defense against humans that I know" and, on the other, as the means that allow the speaker to be "always" waiting for his beloved. This sense of eternity is likewise not found in the poem. While the phrase "defense against humans" is probably a simple sign of woodchuck identity, the context of the note also suggests it to be a defense against other people, which, in a standard critical interpretation of the poem as a comic allegory, would enter as a prominent fact, linked up with the allusion to war, pestilence, and common sense.

Interestingly, the warning whistle in the poem is altogether misinterpreted as being whistling "to calm myself." This error is part of the overall exaggerated sense of amorous privacy perceived by the respondent. Accordingly, the other animals alluded to in the opening of the poem become "neighbors" in this transcription, suggesting a community more intimate than a group of animals who merely suffer a common threat. This emphasis on private coziness and community completely replaces the speaker's prominent self-congratulation for his own cleverness, which so stood out for respondent C. The only such reference is to the "foolish ones" who do not realize what precautions they must take in order to make up for their small size. Even here, the thought of self-congratulation is minimized and in no way constitutes gloating over the others.

The distortion in respondent E's restatement reaches an even greater level of generality. Though the love theme appears, here toward the end and thus more like the poem, the feeling of interpersonal conversation transforms the literal sense of the poem directly into the allegorical, and the woodchuck's conversation is framed as a mere simile: "Kind of crawl into a hole like a groundhog does." Here again it is likely that the opening lines of E's restatement are taken from a response to material found toward the end of the poem—the speaker's analogy citing war, pestilence, and loss of common sense.* However, this transference emphasizes the human reality that E sees in the poem. To E, to her feelings, that is, the woodchuck imagery is ancillary or merely illustrative, as if there were no question at all in her mind that the human situation is primary. In the service of this certainty, a complete fabrication enters the restatement in the form of "apple pie or my first really nice kiss." Here too we see the influence of the perceptions of the end of the poem on the restatements of the

---

*I call attention to the natural tendency of readers to see the work in terms of one overriding thought they perceive in the poem and then to reconstruct the poem according to this thought. This tendency is one of the subjective bases of the discussion in the next chapter, "Deciding on Literary Importance."

beginning. In the third paragraph another important fabrication enters in the service of this primary perception: E attributes the loss of common sense to herself—or to the speaker—and declares the speaker's perception of this loss to be his projection onto the outside world. In the poem, of course, as most readers agreed, the loss of common sense is definitely taking place in the world outside the woodchuck. This interpolation, therefore, suggests that the speaker felt a personal guilt in addition to his impatience with the troubles of the world. E then has the speaker conquer this guilt and reject the lesser thoughts of pies and kisses and return in capital letters to "YOU." Finally, E fabricates a transcendental vision of the whole affair, to "emerge . . . a sound and whole member of this human race, this vast universe, and be there for YOU. . . ."

Let me again stress that these distortions are not errors. Rather, they are personal embellishments of something which E perceived in the poem and which most professional critics would agree is there. In following instructions to write about what the poem says, E felt freest to present what she actually *felt* it to say. Many students, in commenting on their own transcriptions, said that they felt it was just not possible to relay all the feelings they thought were "in" the poem. E did not offer such an apology and we can surmise why: she added many details of her own, details that she sensed were there while reading. These, for her, were no less important than the "real" parts of the poem, which she distorted and exaggerated, since they were the source of her real feeling.

Consider now two final restatements which demonstrate yet different perceptual attitudes:

> F. It is strange and yet awe inspiring what the smarter of the human race can learn from the animal world.
>
> The smaller species of animals seem to have a natural instinct for self-preservation. Some of them can use a shelving bank or a rotting plank as camouflage instead of immenseness for protection. A somewhat wiser animal, the woodchuck, uses his ability to burrow to fashion escape routes when danger approaches. He sits near these routes as if he were really exposed, ready to flee the moment the alarm is sounded by a lookout. He certainly isn't stupid enough to stick around and enter into a dangerous situation or even watch it, but waits in his refuge until all signs of danger pass—signs such as war, pestilence, or loss of common sense, common among man.
>
> If man stays alive for another year, against the "dangers" he can create, it is only because he has built safeguards against danger, as the woodchuck builds burrows. Man too is small compared to the dangers surrounding him, but he too can learn to build crevices for protection.

G. Everyone needs one place to which he can go for a little solitude, for a little security, from the anxieties that swirl around him. Maybe there is a need to really hide from danger, and maybe it is only a need to have a place to sit and think, to ponder over the dynamism around him. But either way, there is a need for a personal place to go. It follows that old adage: "A man's home is his castle." It implies privacy. It implies security. It hints that a man needs a place to call his own, to which he can retreat. In his own fortress, whether large or small, he can sit and watch, and think about what's "out there" and how it will affect him.

And it doesn't really matter where his retreat is, or how it is built. It need not be complicated and complex. Nor need it be elaborate. The security it affords is not in its design; it is the suitability that counts. One man might indeed need a castle. Another might find his "castle" in one small room. Yet another will find that perfect reflection can be found on a garden path—alone and undisturbed. It matters not where that castle is, or what it really looks like. It is the sense of security that is important, and when that security is felt, when a man can step back for a moment and take a look at the outside from the in, and yet have a feeling of assurance of his position, he has a real castle.

This personal place can be pretty important to a man. There are often certain danger signals that tell him it is time for a retreat into seclusion from the world around him. There is no one signal; every man has his own. For some it may take the form of tension, or anxiety. For others it may be an inability to understand or combat the forces that affect him. Real fear of something, too, can be the signal. Regardless of what that signal is, he knows it and hears it, and when he does, it's time to make haste for the retreat. Now is the occasion, and there is the place, to think and reflect. Let the others pass by the castle. It is time for him to turn and enter it.

He would be at no small disadvantage did he not have this place of retreat. But in it he has a sort of friend. His castle compensates for some things he may be lacking—immediate self-assurance, quickness in decision, and so on. But when he hears the danger signal and can take a step back and pause, and look, at ease in the comfort and security of his castle, he is able to see things more clearly, to reason more logically. Without his refuge he might indeed be in real trouble. The castle might be thought of as a movie house. When he finds himself in trouble—real trouble—it is to his theater he goes and, alone, snaps on the projector. Here he can really focus in.

I place these two restatements in a religious or philosophical category, since their reflective moods contrast with the more emotional senses present in the other restatements. The important feature of these renditions is that one cannot locate a single line in the poem from which these can be said to "take off." The centers of emphasis here are on the interpretive abstraction itself.

Respondent F views the poem as a homily on the human instinct for self-preservation and uses the woodchuck's situation as a kind of scriptural text for the homily. Even the presentation of this text is in the service of the homily. The characterization of the woodchuck as a "wiser animal" is the respondent's own interpolated detail, since the speaker of the poem does not in fact call himself wiser than the other animals. The restatement also shifts the poem from the first to the third person and without explicit notice says that the protagonist of the poem is mankind and not the woodchuck, a kind of shift which helps create the homiletic mood. The contrast between what is wise and what is "stupid" calls attention to what mankind "can learn" (a phrase used twice in the restatement) from the animals, rather than to an element in the woodchuck's personal sense of self-congratulation. Finally, in what is perhaps the one line used as a take-off point, F finds in the "war, pestilence, and the loss of common sense" proof that man is the subject here, since these are "common among man." This homiletic mood is what this respondent sees that the poem *actually says* and is not given as a reinterpretation. Again, this is not an error, but an important form of individuated perception created by the particular biases of the reader.

G's restatement is obviously the most radically distorted of all. In a case like this, there is very little doubt that the individual's preoccupations interfered with perception. Our question is, however, whether this is really an interference. All of the abstractions, which make almost no reference to the actual words of the poem, do in fact refer to particular parts of the poem, and G's restatement follows it just as the others do.

G creates his own theme—"a man's home is his castle"—and manipulates its specified meaning according to what he thinks he sees in the poem. The choice of possible refuges found in the poem, for example, is translated in G's second paragraph into his own set of choices—a "small room" or a "garden path." The overall mood of the restatement is reflective rather than homiletic, and the main thought of each paragraph is redundant. The first paragraph is the need itself; the second, the irrelevance of what form the castle is; the third, the nature of its importance; and the fourth, its use as a refuge. The only word in this restatement whose idea is taken from the poem is "signal," which the respondent enlarges considerably from its original use. In general G sees the poem in a metonymical relationship to a much larger reality: it is to him but a minor example of a major concern of his own life. While it is true that G does not say that this is his own concern, I cannot otherwise explain his elaborate effort to make his ideas clear. G is trying, harder than most of the respondents, to make clear what is in his own mind. The metaphorical nature of G's restatement demonstrates its personal nature, as well as G's own eagerness to take advantage of this assignment to express himself. Under normal circumstances, this respondent might be setting himself up for a torrent of criticism, with an invidious comparison between his work and that of, say, respondent A. From our standpoint, however, it is far more important to note that both G and A failed to take into account that one line, "I will be there for you, my dear."

Although one cannot say for sure, one can almost tell the reasons for the omission—in A's case, an excessive detachment from the poem, and in G's case, an excessive eagerness to appropriate the poem to some larger preoccupation of his own. The content of the line would bear this supposition out: it tells of a close relationship between the speaker and his hearer, and neither respondent, for the reasons I have suggested, was able to perceive this relationship. Their own frames of mind at the time of reading did not allow this particular perception.

In class it is important to resist the temptation to criticize such restatements, and instead to emphasize two particular things. First, that each respondent does "see" something in the poem that everyone else can also see is "there." Second, that each person has a special way of seeing that something, which gives it its own personalized character, so that it could be called a "distortion." But this is just the word that should be avoided. This "distortion" is not that, but is instead an expression of personal style and concern. Each respondent should be alerted to his particular style of perception and should be urged to ask himself, Why do I think I saw the poem in just this way? Is there anything I know about myself that might explain this particular kind of perception? The respondent, in other words, should be asked to objectify himself deliberately, to look at his own work as an object in this disciplined context. The motive is created because *his own* work is the object of examination, while the whole question of a grade evaluation is rendered irrelevant.

The so-called "mistakes" are part of an individual's perceptual style, just as are the omissions, the exaggerations, and the superfluous material that almost everyone will insert. The purpose of having everyone resay the poem is not to see that prose can't say what verse can say, or even that another person can't say exactly what Frost said. These things should be so obvious that they are hardly worth spending time on. The purpose, rather, is to understand how and why each person sees differently.

Most people do already know that each sees differently, but few are willing to look into the question of how and why this is the case.

The Affective Response

The second level of feeling, so to speak, is an affective response. Here the respondent, more than just telling what he sees in the poem or what he thinks the poet says (though this kind of information inevitably is used), describes the actual affect he felt while reading the poem. Consider Robert Frost's "Away!" and two affective responses to it.

Away!

Now I out walking
The world desert,
And my shoe and my stocking
Do me no hurt.

I leave behind
Good friends in town.
Let them get well-wined
And go lie down.

Don't think I leave
For the outer dark
Like Adam and Eve
Put out of the Park

Forget the myth.
There is no one I
Am put out with
Or put out by.

Unless I'm wrong
I but obey
The urge of a song:
I'm—bound—away!

And I may return
If dissatisfied
With what I learn
From having died.

H. Upon reading the first five stanzas of this poem, I felt an identification with the speaker. His sense of adventure and individualism pushed him out of the confines of ordinary existence and I admired his sense of freedom. It was like a compulsion to leave the familiar and find answers to searching questions among the unfamiliar. However, as I reached the last stanza and realized that the speaker's journey was one into death, I became sad. Since there is no physical return from death, the speaker could not relate his discoveries to anyone. Although death may be an adventure, it is not one to be shared with those left behind. Therefore, my feelings after reading the entire poem are somewhat uncertain since they would tend to sway two different directions if the poem was entirely as it seemed from the beginning or if it followed the same tone as the last stanza throughout.

I. "Away!" by Robert Frost makes me feel that the poet is a man who is free of those inhibitions that might make someone else feel guilty at leaving home for a simple change of scene. This feeling is a good one, because when I read this poem, I know how it would feel to be free of guilt in doing something unconventional—just to walk off to a new place. Frost has made his leaving of his friends to go to a new place very attractive; it seems that he is not relieved to be going, but that he is glad to be himself doing what he is doing. I felt, along with Frost, no regret at leaving because he. has left no scores to settle, ahead or behind him, in his journey. This sense of freedom that I detect in the poem is hard to precisely define— I feel the urge to wander to new places with the poet; I want to share the satisfaction at having set out anew with a healthy satisfaction at what I am doing. That feeling of no regrets for anything done in the past that I find in the poem gives me a sense of continuity—there is no finality in what Frost is doing. The past, I feel, is not lost, but can be regained by coming back to it. But the poet is not unaware that change will occur; he is free of worrying that things won't be satisfactory; he just wants to wander around with himself and think for a while. Frost's wanting to do this, and having the courage to do it, even in a poem, evoked my admiration; it makes me glad that this sort of freedom exists; it made me feel good. And, I'm glad that Frost said that he had died by leaving this place, because leaving for somewhere else is probably all that death is, and no one ever said that he isn't free to come back. The freedom is the good feeling and the solidity of this poem.

These two responses represent two different degrees of affective involvement. Response H is about as rudimentary as one can get and still offer an affective report. There are only three personal statements of rather limited scope: "I felt an identification with the speaker," "I admired his sense of freedom," and "I became sad." In the first statement the feeling is hardly even named, though one might infer it from reading the poem. The second statement might help explain the first, though one wonders if admiration for someone else's sense of freedom amounts to an identification with that person. And the last statement shows a change of mood from a hopeful one to a depressed one. It is important to see these statements as interconnected. The identification with the speaker is actually an identification with what is perceived as the speaker's wish for freedom. For the respondent this wish is defeated by the last stanza, and so she is "sad" as a result of this relatively simple frustration. The affects reported by this respondent are not elaborated with further affect or analogy, but with a presumably rational explanation based on the facts of life and death. This response, therefore, is a kind of minimum. It is of course possible that H felt more deeply and complexly, but there is no way of telling this without further discussion from her. I offer it here to show just how limited an affective report can be and still reveal some of the process by which this affect can appear.

Restatement I, while still only naming feelings, does so in a much more specific and recognizably experiential form: "I know how it would feel to be free of guilt in doing something unconventional." This freedom from guilt develops in terms of a specific activity: "I feel the urge to wander to new places," "I want to share the satisfaction." So strong is this particular feeling of abandon, which leads to a similar admiration we found in restatement H, that the thought of death, even, is reduced in importance to "leaving for somewhere else." While there is a good deal of redundancy in this response, as in restatement G, there is an overall sense of its mood. This mood is not simply guiltlessness, abstractly or even behaviorally, but it derives from having found a kindred spirit in the poet. The respondent manufactures a relationship with him in order to express her feelings. It is not merely an identification, however, because the respondent says, "I feel the urge to wander to new places *with the poet*." It is actually an imaginary relationship, which gradually resolves itself into a discussion of that other person, the speaker/poet. There is an important piece of knowledge to be gained from this response: *the expression of affect naturally leads to its explanation in terms of relationship.*

Identification with a speaker or protagonist, present in both of these affective responses, is a rather common event in one's reading experience, perhaps the most basic event in our "getting into" a work of literature. In our responses, we observe it coming into play, unsolicited, as it were, as part of a natural expression of how we feel. It provides an important corroboration of our principle of evaluating associative responses, as we will discuss shortly. In response I, the pleasure reported by the respondent is not guiltlessness by itself, but guiltlessness as the respondent imagines it to be also experienced by an important person, the poet. The thoughts of the poem gain a major additional importance through the respondent's having imagined them offered by a very important person. Think, for example, of the ordinary childhood situation where a child does something he thinks may be disapproved by his parent, like riding a bicycle on a dangerous street. But instead of disapproval, the parent says, "Oh, yes, I used to like to do that when I was young also." Together the act and the parent create a great positive affect in the child. Yet, it is the parent's words which are the key to producing the good feeling. Their action is the determining influence in the production of the affect associated with a particular experience, in the same way as peer group response so frequently validates all kinds of adolescent behavior that would never be tolerated in normal adult life.

Consider this principle now in the following affective response to Frost's "On Going Unnoticed."

On Going Unnoticed

As vain to raise a voice as a sigh
In the tumult of free leaves on high.
What are you in the shadow of trees
Engaged up there with the light and breeze?

Less than the coral-root you know
That is content with the daylight low,
And has no leaves at all of its own;
Whose spotted flowers hang meanly down.

You grasp the bark by a rugged pleat,
And look up small from the forest's feet
The only leaf it drops goes wide,
Your name not written on either side.

You linger your little hour and are gone,
And still the woods sweep leafily on,
Not even missing the coral-root flower
You took as a trophy of the hour.

J.   When I hear the shrill whirr of a siren, an innate kind of fear drives me to the window to peer out at the passing ambulance. And as I see the flash of red and chrome speed by, a sadness mixes with my momentary fear. For a few brief minutes a stonelike tenseness hangs in my breast and throat. Then the sight and sound are gone and so is the fearful sadness. Or when I read or hear that someone as young as me has died—although I do not even know the victim—I feel the same intense sadness. Again it is momentary. Quickly other, less significant details of everyday life subdue the feeling.

This same mixture of sadness and fear strikes me as I read Robert Frost's "On Going Unnoticed." I feel a hard knotted lump of something inside me as I read. No matter how many times I read it I have this same reaction—intense sadness, the kind of gloominess that comes quickly and lasts only a short time. This sadness is not the same kind that I feel when I think of my dying father. It is rather the same unhappiness I feel every time I discover something not really close to me alone, but something universal, that I dislike but can't change.

Perhaps because I have had the same thoughts before myself, but always shoved them out of my mind, my first feeling is that Frost is right. Also like the ambulance or the unexpected death of a young person, the reading of this poem fills me with fear. I feel that the poet is correct, and I am suddenly reminded that it could, at any time, be me who rushes headlong into some unknown extinction, only to be "unnoticed." "On Going Unnoticed" hits me with a powerful blow at the time I read it and for the few minutes I think about it afterward. Then ambiguously when the book is closed I convince myself that some other you may "linger your little hour and be gone," but not me.

Yet the truth is that I still feel, without any great mass of data for proof, that Frost is right. And in the future when I come across this idea that man is "less than the coral-root," that the "forest" will not miss him, or even remember his name when he leaves, the sadness and fear will be there. It will again be momentary, but it will be there.

Finally as I read the poem I feel it is important because it is true. Although it will return, this feeling too is short lived. I can easily dismiss it and plunge into the more insignificant thoughts and actions that make up my life.

We cannot deny, at the outset, that J is especially articulate and that such a special skill or fluency in language might here be the source of that "something extra" not found in the other responses. Without exploring the issue in great depth, however, I will only say that my experience has been that "verbal skill" is not an independent talent, and that it is not possible for us teachers to distinguish between this skill and a person's strong desire to express himself. I have seen many students with lesser vocabulary and fluency compose equally vivid and powerful statements.

We observe in the opening paragraph the almost automatic impulse to explain the affect in detail and with more than one example. While these analogies may be classified as associations, they are more important as ways to help the reader recreate that feeling than as means for determining what aspect of the personality is involved. That is the basic functional difference between an affective analogy and an associative analogy. The analogies themselves involve others—the victim in the ambulance or the peer who has died—the speaker's relationship to these people being purely subjective. Nevertheless, these human elements in the analogies take us one step further toward the level of associative analogy involving important relationships.

In the second paragraph we actually do see an important associative analogy, though it is presented rather obliquely. The "intense sadness" described by J "is not the same kind that I feel when I think of my dying father." There must obviously be an important truth in J's manifest denial. I take it, however, that the sad thoughts of her dying father are constant and nagging rather than intense and transient. More fundamentally, however, the denial only covers up the real analogy, which aims to express the feeling that some very important part of her emotional investment in life is threatened by both her dying father and the intense sadnesses described in the opening paragraph. The remainder of the response does reveal this analogy. What J terms "something universal" turns out to be something very personal indeed. In the third paragraph we observe the by-now-familiar habit of the reader's assuming a certain intimacy with the poet/speaker. J observes that the "poet is correct" "perhaps because I have had the same thoughts before myself." That is, the poet is "correct" because he feels the way I do. The way J particularly feels, we now learn, is that she herself feels she may "linger [her] little hour and be gone," just like the ambulance victim, the dead peer, or the dying father. J then expresses this very personal feeling in the "universal" sense she mentioned earlier—that it is "man," the species, rather than her, the individual, who is "less than the coral-root." By the end of the response, J emphasizes the "truth" of this feeling rather than its depth or intensity. Even for this articulate and responsive young woman, the intense and important personal feeling must be justified by its truth or universality and is not allowed to stand by itself, even though it is very plain both to us and to her that the foundation of this truth or correctness lies in the fact that she was willing and able to make it apply to her own life.

In spite of the complexity of the foregoing response, its analysis led to a more complex understanding of it as a feeling, a personal sense of mortality which, though transient, is real in all of us. Indirectly, the personality of the respondent is manifest in such a response, but it is really only the quality and terms of a single affect which we know about in any detail. The response demonstrates the multiplicity of directions in which even a single, though important, affect may be elaborated and, in an important sense, "explained" by the different sorts of analogies brought to bear. The opening portions of the response show some kind of mystery regarding what the respondent actually feels about "going unnoticed," and it is not until the concluding portions of the response that we discover how important a feeling she really has, and how many aspects of her previous experience are stimulated

by the affect derived from a single poetic experience. If we limit
the discussion of emotional response to affect alone, this response
represents about the furthest we can go. Nevertheless, it is clear
from this response that the pursuit of one's affective reaction
naturally and automatically leads to the study of an associative
response.

The Associative Response

Mending Wall

Something there is that doesn't love a wall,
That sends the frozen-ground-swell under it,
And spills the upper boulders in the sun;
And makes gaps even two can pass abreast.
The work of hunters is another thing:
I have come after them and made repair
Where they have left not one stone on a stone,
But they would have the rabbit out of hiding,
To please the yelping dogs. The gaps I mean,
No one has seen them made or heard them made,
But at spring mending-time we find them there.
I let my neighbor know beyond the hill;
And on a day we meet to walk the line
And set the wall between us once again.
We keep the wall between us as we go.
To each the boulders that have fallen to each.
And some are loaves and some so nearly balls
We have to use a spell to make them balance;
'Stay where you are until our backs are turned!'
We wear our fingers rough with handling them.
Oh, just another kind of outdoor game.
One on a side. It comes to little more:
There where it is we do not need the wall:
He is all pine and I am apple orchard.
My apple trees will never get across
And eat the cones under his pines, I tell him.
He only says, 'Good fences make good neighbors.'
Spring is the mischief in me, and I wonder
If I could put a notion in his head:
'Why do they make good neighbors? Isn't it
Where there are cows? But here there are no cows.
Before I built a wall I'd ask to know
What I was walling in or walling out,
And to whom I was like to give offense.
Something there is that doesn't love a wall,
That wants it down.' I could say 'Elves' to him,
But it's not elves exactly, and I'd rather

He said it for himself. I see him there
Bringing a stone grasped firmly by the top
In each hand, like an old-stone savage armed.
He moves in darkness as it seems to me,
Not of woods only and the shade of trees.
He will not go behind his father's saying,
And he likes having thought of it so well
He says again, 'Good fences make good neighbors.'

1   K. "Something there is that doesn't love a wall." I remember when I was young and how I was always sent to my room for punishment of something I had done wrong. I hated being sent to my room, not in the beginning, of course, because I always thought I'd get even with my Mom and show her that I could have a lot of fun in there. As the hours went by, though, I usually ran out of things to do and therefore I would always try to think of a good story to tell sweet ole Dad about how mean Mom had been to me. I just hated those four blank walls; I guess that's because I saw them so often.

2   . . . The gaps I mean,
No one has seen them made or heard them made,
But at spring mending-time we find them there.

This reminds me of the making-up time with my boyfriend. At times I can see us drifting apart from one another, having little spats over a trivial subject. This drifting apart usually is not completely revealed until after the climactic fight, when we tell each other how rotten the other one is and also the long list of faults he has. But after the big fight, usually about a week, he comes over and we laugh about the stupidity of the fight. Making up or "mending" our disputes and troubles were fun. I guess its because things go so well for awhile after the fight. We're each very nice to each other.

3   Another thing along the same line that this quote reminds me of is how my boyfriend and I appreciate each other more and get along so much better when we do not see each other very often or when we are a considerable distance apart. We seem to enjoy each other's company much more and have a fewer number of fights. I feel that sometimes it's better not to be around someone you care about a lot, because if you're around them all the time you tend to pick out all their faults. Of course, its usually because you picture this person as being perfect and that is usually what you try to expect from them instead of overlooking these faults.

4   And on a day we meet to walk the line
And set the wall between us once again.

This brings back the memories of the neighborhood gang fights. It wasn't really a "gang fight" like in the movies or on television shows, but what I mean by a gang fight is a whole group of kids would get together and decide that they weren't going to play with one certain person. Of course, every once in a while that poor creature ended up being yourself, and that was when it was really bad. It always seemed like there was only one person that never got "ganged-up" against and that was my neighbor. I guess you could call her the "brains" of the mob. She was really a trouble-maker, the more I look back at the situation. Well, anyway, whenever it was my turn to be hated, I always got my notice when Carol started drawing "the property line." The funniest part of this whole situation was that her mother always got into the fight. The line always went "you better keep off of my property or I'll call the poleece"—her mother had a French accent. It was really ridiculous! They even set up a guard duty to make sure I wouldn't cross their property— all the kids in the neighborhood took a different shift. Thank goodness for public sidewalks and streets! These fights or gang-ups happened about once every two months to the same person. Usually after about a week of the whole deal, Carol would come over and dumb ole me or whoever the fight was against would, of course, get "buddy-buddy" with her and then was the shift of the scene to some other poor soul. These fights seemed to follow a cycle; I'm only glad that summer vacations last only three months! To look back at the good old days really makes you see the stupidity of it all, but what is funnier is to see the young neighborhood kids today holding the same "gang fights" with the "property line" disputes.

To each the boulders that have fallen to each.
And some are loaves and some so nearly balls
We have to use a spell to make them balance:
'Stay where you are until our backs are turned!'

The camping days of my life and the experiences were horrible when they occurred but funny to talk about afterwards. The words "boulders" and "balls" remind me of the overnight camp-out in the woods. At camp we had what was called a "family"—half boys and half girls with a couple of counselors. Well, my "family" slept out in the woods one evening. In preparing for the evening, the boys were to rig up a tarp for us (the girls) to sleep under. They did a beautiful job of rigging the tarp, making sure that it was up securely by placing big logs on it in key spots where they would supposedly not get loose and drop. Well, at least that was the main idea, but during the middle of the night one of these logs worked itself loose and fell—directly onto my head. Now, you can see probably very well how the words "boulder" and "balls" remind me of this experience. It was quite a surprise to be awakened during the middle of the night with a thump on the head which left a beautiful bump! In fact it was rather upsetting, especially when you are supposed to have a tarp over your head for protection! At first, of course— considering the time of night—I had no idea about what was happening, but immediately afterwards I did manage to become both upset and scared. It was like "Chicken Little" and "the sky is falling" story. I kept thinking that it was a dream; the only thing that could make me think different was the evidence on my forehead—the bump.

6   He is all pine and I am apple orchard
      My apple trees will never get across
      And eat the cones under his pines,

When I came across this line in the poem it brought back memories of when a group of us would always try to sneak over to the apple orchard behind my house and steal apples. It probably sounds stupid, but sometimes I thought it was fun to get caught picking the apples, because when we ran to get away from the old woman who was chasing us, we could think of a real juicy story of how we managed to sneak away with Mrs. Larsen's apples while she tried to run after us and catch us. Sometimes we used to have wars in the trees. We would climb up in the trees—one row for each side, to make sure that we wouldn't hit our own players—and throw apples at each other. What a riot! Sometimes we managed to catch one of our foes off guard and off balance and knock them right out of the tree with only one "little" apple. One thing we were lucky about when we had these wars was that no one got hurt, especially when they got knocked out of the trees. That part made the game a little better.

7   Before I built a wall I'd ask to know
      What I was walling in or walling out,
      And to whom I was like to give offense

The three lines above remind me of mental blocks. Sometimes when I am walking outside, my mind drifts off into some world or on something I need to get done. This is all I am concentrating on, and this is what gets me in a lot of trouble with my friends because when they pass me and speak to me, they usually receive no reply because I usually don't hear or see them. The next time I see them they tell me how stuck-up I am because I don't speak to them while passing on the street. In short, to try to apply this problem with the above, I build a wall which closes out my friends sometimes which then gives them an offensive feeling toward me.

8   Another instance of about the same type of situation is walling out your friends from activities that you are in or walling out the concern for their feelings and the possibility of hurting them in this way which could possibly result in ill-feelings towards you.

9   Through this poem, memories of good and bad times of my childhood were brought back. One experience, in particular, was the "property line" affair. This seems to show the foolishness of walls or lines separating people—it can cause ill feelings, and sometimes walls are built to stop persisting quarrels. The "Berlin Wall," for instance, was built to keep the East Berliners from going over to the better life plus it walled out the possible chance of jealousy of seeing how well the others are living.

10   This wall could also mean the wall of racial prejudice and narrow-mindedness of so many people. The United States especially is having many problems with civil rights. There are so many whites and colored people that are so narrow-minded that these are the ones

that usually cause the riots and killings. Another point to bring in is that so many people do things without thinking about them first, such as the colored trying to get their rights and the ways they go about getting them. Many whites, in the treating of the civil rights problems, only follow present behavior lines of their fathers. They do not try to think things out for themselves to see if they can find an answer to their problems, but all they do is just go by the ways and rules of their predecessors. The line that I am going to quote can show more exactly what I mean by racial prejudice and narrow-minded people.

> He moves in darkness as it seems to me,
> Not of woods only and the shade of trees.

K's response is almost all association. There are numerous thoughts, in the usual sense, and numerous affects present, though these are always connected with the associations rather than directly to the poem. The authenticity of the response is documented by the fluency of the associations, their conversational presentation, their line-by-line sequence, and most importantly, by the single theme they present. This theme, however, is not manifest, but I will try to show that it is prominent in the response and that it provides a far stronger sense of the reader's experience and relationship with the poem than any of the affective responses we have just studied. I will also note that this response is an excellent example of the use of important interpersonal relationships. Each association is characterized by either an interpersonal or group experience, and the response culminates with thoughts on political and social situations which K finds analogous to the more personal material she has discussed.

While the response is organized so that each association seems to be to particular lines, this is not altogether the case: the association is usually to a part of a line or to a word or specific image. It will become clear how these apparent disjunctions add up to a surprisingly unified response.

One behavioral schema dominates the response. Let us call it, "K, the victim." In paragraph 1 she is sent to her room by her mother. In paragraph 4 she is the frequent victim of the neighborhood ringleader-bully, whose mother partakes in the bullying. In paragraph 5 a log falls on her head. In paragraph 6 she is the victim of Mrs. Larsen's wrath, for picking her apples. Paragraph 7 finds her friends chewing her out for being "stuck-up." In paragraph 9 she speaks of victimization by the Berlin wall, and in the last paragraph, she speaks of the various kinds of victims resulting from the struggle for equal rights.

We may say that this theme expands as the response proceeds.

K begins with a mother-daughter scene, goes through a boyfriend-girlfriend episode and commentary, then into various kinds of groups until, at the end, she reaches public life. One can all too easily describe this expansion as "growth of social awareness." While this may be part of what is happening, it is certainly not the whole story. Beginning in paragraph 6, the central point of the victim stories changes. There, for the first time, K openly names her own aggression as the cause: "A group of us would always try to sneak over to the apple orchard behind my house and steal apples." I note for future reference that this important change takes place in response to a part of the poem which affirms the separateness of the apple orchards and the pines. The poem's statement of stasis provokes K into revealing the key personal fact that her own aggression may have played a part in her victimizations. The line acts as a kind of invitation to K to "step over" the peaceful situation. This she does by bringing out a tale of her own aggression in what heretofore has been a series of personal complaints.

Clearly, K reports these events as if the theft and the deliberate fun in getting caught were only a game, and Mrs. Larsen is portrayed as a kind of villain who interferes with children's play. In fact, she is made a villain to begin with in order to create the game of stealing apples. Theft is not the only interesting aspect to this game: "Sometimes we used to have wars in the trees," in which, obviously, K was an active participant, some of the pleasures of which included "catching one of our foes off guard and off balance and knocking them right out of the tree with only one 'little' apple." The whole activity was, metaphorically, "a riot." There is very little doubt, however, that this is all kid stuff and simply came to mind with the poetic use of the term "apple orchard."

In the light of K's remarks in paragraphs 9 and 10, however, this association is not only kid stuff. There, where she is trying to find an overview for all the associations she has presented, she cites the "property line" affair as the outstanding association, no doubt because it was the most personally painful of the various things she remembered. Instead of mentioning this pain again, she calls such lines or walls "foolishness." She then rises above not only her own pain but political reality as well by tearing down the Berlin wall as a similar foolishness. This international allusion, however, relates as much to the "war" waged between the trees in paragraph 6 as it does to the property line disputes. In paragraph 7, moreover, K describes how she erects her own "wall": "I built a wall which closes out my friends sometimes which then gives them an offensive feeling toward me." There is reason to believe, in other words, that in addition to being a victim, K does harbor a private guilt over being the aggressor and the wallbuilder, a guilt overcome by the moralistic disquisition against walls.

Her last paragraph is most revealing in this regard. Again there is a moralistic declaration against the narrow-mindedness of racially prejudiced people. To her, it is *both* white and "colored people" whose narrow-mindedness "usually causes riots and killings." She then singles out "the colored" (with the "people" now missing from the phrase) as using means "to get their rights" "without thinking about [these means] first." Finally, though it is far from clear, K's last quotation suggests an ironic identification of narrow-mindedness with "darkness." The poem itself nowhere alludes to a "color" question, but K's allusion to it combines interestingly with that final quotation to make it rather clear that she is a member of the white majority, complete with its color-coded imagery about knowledge and ignorance, good and evil, light and darkness. And this majority is suspiciously similar to the gang and its ringleader that selected her for its periodic assaults.

In addition to this mild suggestion that K takes some pride in or takes refuge in being on the stronger side, another theme running counter to the victim's sentiments appears in paragraphs 2 and 3, where she is discussing her relationship with her boyfriend. Ostensibly, paragraph 2 shows the association to be about "spring mending-time," with the analogy to mending a relationship. However, paragraph 3 casts a different light on things. K reports that she and her boyfriend "get along so much better when we do not see each other very often or when we are a considerable distance apart." This is not an uncommon situation, especially in relationships between younger people. However, I think there is a connection between K's value of separateness here, her "mental blocks" in paragraph 7 where she mentally separates herself from her friends passing her on the street, and the ever so faint value of racial separateness in paragraph 10. We should also note in this regard that when she was sent to her room alone, as she reports in paragraph 1, "I always thought . . . that I could have a lot of fun in there," but that she had to finally call on "sweet ole Dad" to bail her out.

In pointing out possible counterthemes to what I am calling the "main theme" in the response, I am underscoring the emotional dialectic that takes place in this, and, as I have come to see, in almost every response. That is, there are always certain patterns of conscious assertion, while there are other, less obvious patterns that reveal another side to the assertions. It is quite obvious that such a dialectic does not take place consciously, since the respondent only picks out things in the poem, seemingly at random, which strike important emotional chords. In this response I think the dialectic amounts to the following situation: "I surely don't like being a victim so much, yet I seem to have a distinct sympathy with or perhaps envy of the victimizer. This is something of a problem for me, so perhaps it is best just to withdraw to my own room or mind, where this is no longer a problem." This "withdrawal" takes place in the final paragraphs in her discussion of the narrow-mindedness of both sides of the equal rights dispute. This is of course a very familiar pattern, often found in public life in the name of reason and compromise, but which, if viewed from a personal basis, avoids the problems of commitment and obviates the risks of getting involved and taking a stand.

K views the poem as being about walls, if we are to judge from her more reflective discussion at the end of the response and from the kinds of things in the poem to which she responded. Her overall sympathy is with a speaker who she takes to be, so to speak, against walls. While she agrees in paragraph 1 that she in fact "doesn't love a wall," she subsequently offers associations of pleasures in crossing walls surreptitiously, and even of building them herself, as in paragraphs 3 and 7. Ultimately, it turns out, she "doesn't love a wall," but not because they are intrinsically a bad thing. Rather, she would prefer not to cope with their meaning and function, good or bad, and she takes comfort in the speaker's own judgment that people who think that "good fences make good neighbors" "move in darkness."

K, like most of the other respondents we have studied, identifies with the speaker, though she doesn't say so directly. Instead, due to the associative nature of her response, she uses the homiletic pronouncements in the poem as documentation for her views. As a critical posture, this is not new, since we are almost forced to "play along" with the speaker. But numerous critical discussions of this poem in class have shown that one need not sympathize or identify with this speaker. Some student almost always asks, "Well, if this guy doesn't like walls, why does he take the initiative: 'I let my neighbor know beyond the hill'?" At this point the whole problem of the interesting relationship between the speaker and his neighbor is exposed. A whole range of new perceptions of the poem appears, and attention moves away from walls to the speaker's attitude toward his neighbor, and toward whoever is listening to him in the poem.

The other, more personal and psychological theme is also implicit in K's response. It surfaces in academic criticism as the theme of "tradition," and is based on the speaker's remark that the neighbor "will not go behind his father's saying." To be sure, the theme of tradition is only inferred from the fact that the neighbor is old and that, according to the speaker, he says what his father said. From these meager facts the neighbor is billed as an establishmentarian dogmatist, played off against the man of enlightened ideas, the speaker. The personal basis of this theme of "tradition" does appear in K's associations, in paragraphs 1, 4, and 6. I am referring to K's reported confrontations with her mother, her neighbor's mother, and Mrs. Larsen. The encounter with the latter ended in success, while those with the former two ended only in humiliation. It is a rather common need of a child, and then especially an adolescent (which K was at the time of this response) to test and defeat the authority of the parents' generation, and usually of the parents themselves. It is because this important personal impulse is at work in K's response that she finds support in the speaker's judgment that his neighbor "moves in darkness." In terms of this particular theme, K's response develops *from* punishment at the hands of her mother, to humiliation at the hands of her neighbor's mother, to a childish victory over Mrs. Larsen, and finally, if figuratively, to a kind of moral victory over the older neighbor in the poem. K appropriates this latter victory to help enunciate her own resentment of the "dark" and "stupid" behavior of her own neighbor, and perhaps of her mother, an even more intimate "neighbor." The presence of this theme in her response helps explain K's own sense of personal enlightenment about political and social affairs, and the expression of such enlightenment in these latter terms provides an acceptable justification for her presentation of such personal material.

This is not a scheme that K cooked up for just this occasion. Rather, it is a relatively common psychological habit of people to shift the discussion to such large terms when they sense that the time has come to dissolve the personal issue altogether, without either stopping the conversation abruptly or drawing a conclusion from the personal issue in its own terms. Such a homiletic windup is an exhortation to oneself, really, framed as if it were a general reflection and a vague exhortation to others.

We should now recognize this habit as the one with which we began our discussion of the elementary presentation of feelings above. At even the simplest level, instead of saying "I like so and so," we say "so and so is nice." In the poem, the speaker criticizes the neighbor, instead of reporting his own irritation. And then K appropriates the common habit. The habit of objectification is fundamental in human mental functioning, and no one does without it. Our point here is that we can observe its subjective function, especially so in these associative responses. There will come a point in almost anyone's response when some form of objectification will come to the rescue to depersonalize the response. Professional criticism, framed as it always is in objective terms, is an institutional form of this universal psychological habit. Beyond a certain point it is assumed feelings cannot be discussed—they are inimical to truth. We now see here in the case of literary response and judgment that truth is not a viable goal, and that we must understand the habit of objectification in its subjective origin.

The associative response, therefore, is the most complex but the most useful form of expressing feelings about literature. It reveals perception, affect, associations, relationships, and finally a patterned presentation of all of these in a way that demonstrates how they are organized in that particular person. Most of all, the associative response shows most clearly that each individual reworks a poem according to the demands of his personality at the time of reading. Some responses show very vividly the effect of the respondent's *current* preoccupations: these preoccupations are frequently a subject of the associations. While this may be true in the foregoing response, it is definitely not clear. But in each response, we may be sure that it in some way represents a combination of the aggregate self-image, and the self-image at the time of reading. My guess is that the boyfriend material and the rebellion material in K's response does represent current preoccupation, for K is an adolescent, where such preoccupations are expectable. If one goes through the steps of understanding perception and affect, the logic of studying associations becomes clear and an experiential basis is formed for the study of the larger process of critical judgment.

Deciding on Literary Importance

The Subjectivity of Critical Judgment

We have seen in our exploration of various kinds of responses that critical judgments are implicit in emotional reactions. As we are well aware, however, the process of making intellectual judgments is always conscious. Indeed, the very fact that judgments are consciously and deliberately made gives them their unique character. Our basic aim here is not to separate these two types of literary reaction, but to show how they are both part of a single and more general process of response, which begins in complete subjectivity and is then transformed into judgments that appear to be objective. The main new fact we are here presenting is that while we are definitely conscious of making self-directed judgments, there is a discoverable causal relationship between the conscious judgment and the earlier subjective reaction. When we are making the judgment, we are necessarily unaware of this key causal relationship. The reasons we think are causing our judgments are really only a part of the complete cause for our making them. Ultimately, the separation of conscious judgment from its subjective roots is false and artificial. Any such deliberate mental act necessarily involves subjective causes and processes. It is this larger and much more general conception of critical judgment that we are trying to demonstrate here.

The Most Important Word in "The Rocking-Horse Winner"

This more general conception of critical judgment forces us to think of it as a judgment of subjective value as opposed to objective fact. The practical presentation of literature under this conception will therefore introduce a new idea that can accommodate this conception, the idea of *literary importance*. Initially, the work of literature is held up to the class as an object, and the class is asked to make certain judgments regarding what is important about the work. The sequence of problems I have used begins by asking for the most important word in the work, then the most important passage, and then the most important feature, whatever it may turn out to be. Whatever sequence is used, the fundamental question is always raised at the very outset: What does one mean by *the most important?* It is immediately clear that each person has a different sense of what "important" means, and the following discussion suggests a method to explore this basic question. Consider now two different essays on "the most important word" in "The Rocking-Horse Winner," by D. H. Lawrence.

Example: Objective Criteria of Importance

1   L.   The most important word in D. H. Lawrence's story "The Rocking-Horse Winner" is "luck," along with its adjective form "lucky." It is the most important word in the story not primarily because it is used many times, but because through its frequent use it comes to play a primary part in denoting the motivations of the two main characters and their basis for interaction; and because this interaction provides the main action of the story, which ends tragically, the word "luck" also comes to denote a false value, a belief in which, when substituted for a belief in the true value of love, constitutes a tragedy in the view of the author.

2   An emphasis on "luck" is present from the beginning of the story, with the statement that "There was a woman who was beautiful, who started with all the advantages, yet she had no luck." Her marriage, which at first seems lucky to her, loses all its meaning; her hopes of economic well-being are also shattered, and this, too, is attributed to a lack of luck: "Though [her husband] had good prospects, these prospects never materialized." She views her children, "thrust upon her," as personifying her unlucky marriage, and communicates to them, without speaking of it, her lack of love for them. At the same time, she communicates to them her view that luck, the lack of which seems to her the main reason for her unhappiness, is a desirable value: "[Luck] is what causes you to have money. If you're lucky you have money. That's why it's better to be born lucky than rich." This statement, juxtaposed with another, "I used to think I was [lucky], before I married. Now I think I am very unlucky indeed," and its implicit expression of lack of love for her children, causes her son, sensing a connection between the two statements, to attempt to secure his mother's love through the gaining of luck.

3   The word "luck" thus assumes a primary position in his aspirations: "He wanted luck, he wanted it, he wanted it." Through an unexplained, seemingly intuitive process, he comes to view the monetary evidence of luck which will satisfy his mother as being attainable for him through the medium of horse racing, which depends for its livelihood upon its supporters' assumptions that they will be lucky. He even comes to place faith in the ability of others to assist him toward his goal on the basis of their seeming luckiness, as can be seen from his stated reason for willingness to allow his uncle to become a partner in his wagering concerns: "you gave me that ten-shilling note I started winning with, so I thought you were lucky."

4   Finally, through the compulsive method of riding his rocking-horse to find the winner of a horse race, he achieves considerable monetary proof of his luckiness with which to impress his mother and thereby to gain her love; however, due to his mother's inability to love, he fails in this larger aim and is destroyed in the process. The main message conveyed to the reader by the story is, therefore, that life and its meaning are destroyed by the substitution of false values for love; and since in this story luck is the false value, the substitution of which for love determines the course of action of the characters, "luck" would seem to be the most important word associated with the story.

5   One important question which follows logically from the preceding discussion of the story is: Since the word "luck," in addition to its important uses in explaining the motives of the characters in the story and the basis for their interaction, may also seem to gain in importance through its relatively frequent use and consequent frequent reinforcement in the mind of the reader, how important is a word to a story if the word seems to possess these same qualities but is used relatively infrequently, or indeed not at all? This question, although needing to be stated to make clear a distinction which may exist between the seeming relative importance to the reader of a frequently used word and that of a less frequently used word, cannot be answered empirically on the basis of this story. However, one generalization which can be made is that a word is important in a work of literature if it is used relatively frequently, and if, through its use, it seems to denote a major motivation for character action and interaction.

This essay was written by an especially articulate sophomore, involved in what he is doing, thoughtful, careful, and intelligent. His point of view with regard to the objectivity of the story is very clear from his opening paragraph: "It is the most important word in the story not primarily because it is used many times, but because through its frequent use it comes to play a primary part in denoting the motivations of the two main characters and their basis of interaction." If I were reading this sentence, and the whole essay for that matter, without regard to the major issues we are exploring, I would say, what a fine insight, let me hear more. L says that luck is a substitute for love in the story and that this substitution constitutes a "tragedy in the view of the author." But now let us consider the assumptions behind this judgment. The most important assumption is that the author is reporting on the interaction of real people and that this author is communicating a judgment that the interaction is tragic. If there were not this assumed separation of the author and his work, the author could not have this "view" of his characters. L follows the common perceptual habit of breaking up his experience of the story into himself, the author, the author's opinion, and the "facts" that the story relates. Assuming these separations, his logic is very strong.

"Luck" is important because it is a false value that obscures the real value for the hero of the story. The real value is, in turn, a "major motivation for the character action and interaction" (paragraph 5). As a result of this reasoning, L says in paragraph 3, "The word 'luck' thus assumes a primary position in his aspirations." But what has happened here? Does this last statement actually follow from the former principle? Is it the *word* "luck" or the "thing" luck that assumes the primary position? The assumption of the story's objectivity, breaking up the story into the categories I enumerated above, leads to the illogical conclusion that the word and not the thing assumes a "primary position in his aspirations." Let us note that L did *not* advance the argument that the word was important to the hero, though one might well advance that argument: Paul does ask his mother about "lucker" and "lucre," and Paul's own repetition of the word "luck" to his mother and his inquiries about it can conceivably be seen as an obsession with a word as well as a "thing." But this is not L's argument. L's clear style affords us the opportunity to see that the false *value* of luck assumed that primary position. His documentation in paragraphs 2 and 3 underscores this argument. Finally, in paragraph 4, L speaks of a "main message conveyed to the reader," and then repeats his central thesis. Again, this statement must partake of the assumption suggested above: the author has a separate "view" that he encodes into a story in order to "tell" the reader this view. Why, one may ask, does the author not just tell the view directly, instead of bothering to write the story? Of course, we need not answer this question, because like the issue of the word getting confused with the thing, it comes out of L's original assumption, the prevailing one, we may note, in contemporary criticism, even though it is never explicitly named as such.

L's attempt to answer the question of the most important word automatically assumes that a word's importance derives from *what it denotes*, and therefore from how this "what" functions in the lives of the imaginary characters. At no point are L's own judgments made explicit. If all the doubts of a personal judgment were made explicit, it would not be possible to mount the argument he did. L *had to* suppress all sense of his subjectivity in order to create the argument. Therefore, in order to produce the socially important illusion of an author, his view, and separate figures *about whom* the author is writing, L makes believe his own judgment plays no part. This illusion is so viable because it places all of the important action "out there" somewhere. If it were not "out there," how in the world could one write about *it*? But this is just the point. In order to avoid writing about what goes on "in here," we make believe we are writing about something "out there" and sneak in our personal judgments under the assumption that everyone else is playing the same game. Only if we abandon this game can we begin discussing the action of a particular word, that is, its action *upon us*, or, in other words, our response to it. Discussion of a word automatically means discussion of its effect upon us, apart from philological considerations.

The question of importance thus changes its focus. Under L's assumptions, importance automatically means "importance in the story." And then criteria are easily adduced for measuring some kind of objective importance. Being intelligent, L evaded the invitation to say that the word is important because it is repeated so often in this story, and thought he was going one step better than the obvious by switching from frequency to value-to-the-hero as the main criterion for judging importance. Indeed, he denies that frequency is a key criterion. A shrewd thinker like L could obviously not bring himself to say that "luck" was an important word because it was used so often; the quantitative nature of such an argument was repugnant to him. This type of argument would indeed be trivial as long as one shares L's assumptions. (After one counts the number of usages, what else can one say?) However, if we use the subjective assumption, the frequency argument becomes much more consequential. Then, we say, a frequently used word makes an especially strong impression on us and guides our attention in a way a less frequently used word would not. By virtue of the fact that we keep reading the same word over and over, a feeling of obsession is created in our reading experience. This feeling is not produced by the author *telling* us anything. Our own capacity for response renders the repetition obsessional. But instead of reporting this subjective fact, we say that the *hero* is obsessed with luck, as is his mother.

The word "luck" could be associated with many things—love among them, as L points out. But its more direct associations are with people. The use of the word in dialogue makes us create a private image of the characters, i.e., this is a woman obsessed with luck, probably because (we infer) she had no love. Paul's final declaration to his mother has its effect through its calling attention to the relationship between mother and son: son claims luck that mother said father was lacking. The action of the word creates in us an attitude toward those using the word. The obsession we may attach to it is then automatically transferred to the figures in the story. But in a respectable essay we do not report that the word made us feel obsessed and made us imagine obsessed characters. We report that the characters are obsessed with luck, thus forgetting that we are speaking of a word, and not a "thing."

Example: Subjective Criteria of Importance

Let us now examine a second essay on the same story, one which is just as intelligent and observant as the first but which uses the subjective assumption to productive ends and is therefore much more conscious of the action of the word rather than the thing.

1   M. A word is important in a work of literature if it can stimulate the reader to use his own imagination and make the story an experience which is totally unique to him. One thing that enables me, as a reader, to truly get involved in a piece of literature is the ability to clearly picture the characters of the story in my mind. Knowing a character's figure and stance is important, but visualizing his face and facial reactions definitely gives me insight to his feelings. A character could be happy, but if the author says, "A broad smile burst across his face," then he seems happier. Likewise a wrinkled brow or a downcast mouth conveys worry or sadness. For this reason, the word "eyes" plays an important role in "The Rocking-Horse Winner." Many of Paul's feelings (uncertainty, coldness, obsession, longing, rejection, victory) are clearly conveyed by various changes in his eyes.

2   An important factor in the story is the coldness that is felt between the mother and her children. It is this lack of feeling that Paul tries to overcome with money. When the author says that no one else could sense this coldness, one feels it might only be occurring in the mother's imagination. However, as soon as Lawrence says, "They read it in each other's eyes," there is an immediate sense of reality in the sentence. I can clearly imagine the frozen and hurt look that is exchanged here, making the feeling more intense and less obscure.

3   Paul's eyes are "blue," "big," and "rather close-set." From this description I get the feeling that Paul is very sensitive and that he

would be very disturbed by the fact that his mother does not love him. Because he appears so sensitive, I can more easily understand his obsession with trying to please his mother. Paul becomes a more realistic character through a simple description of his eyes.

4   The reader can witness Paul's growing obsession by watching his eyes change to fire. Here are the phases he goes through: "unsure eyes," "his eyes had a strange glare," "eyes still flaring," "hot blue eyes," "his eyes were blue fire," "with eyes blazing," "eyes that had an uncanny cold fire," "wild-eyed," "eyes blazing with a sort of madness." The insecurity from a lack of love caused Paul to grow into a fanatic. Instead of just stating this as a fact, Lawrence *describes* the process, allowing the reader to be the active party and interpret the actions himself. That is an important part of literature.

5   Paul's death was certain in my mind as soon as I read that "his eyes were like blue stones." The fire that preceded this was definitely gone, but what replaced it was just as eerie. Once again, through a simple description, the reader experiences a real feeling instead of reading a fact. "Blue stones" enables me to actually see the death instead of vaguely imagining it. The death becomes more vivid.

6   One more character is described by his eyes. I never knew why I mistrusted Bassett until I read the last page of the story. Bassett had "sharp little brown eyes," "glittering, smallish eyes." Being able to picture his face added to his total characterization.

7   Other characters within the story also gained an understanding of Paul through his eyes. The author described Paul as the others saw him, and they always noticed his eyes first. His sisters, his mother, and his uncle all experienced his feelings by looking at his eyes.

8   Because a word is important to *me*, it also is important to the story. Certain "symbolic" words can add much to the theme of the story, but descriptive words of individual characters interest me. Since the eyes allowed me to understand the character more fully, "eyes" was the most important word in the story.

We should first note, in reading through the opening paragraph, how closely M's thoughts resemble what we are now discussing. The remarkable thing is, however, that this "most important word" essay was assigned on the first class meeting of this particular course. M is perhaps a more reflective person than most, I can report, but in the classes preceding the due date there was only the most indirect hint of M's premise. The only conclusion we reached in class discussion was that literature was built with words. The sense of the subjective effect of such words was derived by M altogether by introspection.

In this first paragraph M announces a seemingly commonplace difference between the effect of an image and the effect of a description. However, we should recognize this difference as identical to the one between an affect, happy, and an association, a "broad smile." While M's viewpoint does not exactly revolve about words *per se*, she is able to show how different words are different because of their differing *effects on her*. Finally in that opening paragraph she says that the association of the words (or her most important word) with feelings leads her to feel the word itself to be important. In this way she makes the topic of her essay the actual action of the word.

The example M gives in paragraph 2 is the prototype of her reasoning. For some personal reason we do not know, the sentence "They read it in each other's eyes" is especially vivid for her. But she then reports the palpable subjective effect of this sentence, which made her "clearly imagine the frozen and hurt look that is exchanged here, making the feeling more intense and less obscure." Obviously, not everyone will gain such a clear image from this line, but our point is that there is no doubt from her presentation that the effect is subjective: "I can clearly imagine. . . ."

Her subsequent documentation of the various appearances of "eyes" in the story follows this same logic. We may correctly guess that a certain awareness of Paul's eyes has taken over in M, for she soon seems to be *looking for* the eyes to be future touchstones in her developing response. Even though she speaks objectively of "the reader" in paragraph 4, the important point is that this reader is an "active party" who can "interpret the actions himself." By the end of the essay, M's consciousness of this theme is considerably enlarged, for she notices not only the suspicious "little brown eyes" of Bassett (paragraph 6), but the fact that "other characters within the story also gained an understanding of Paul through his eyes" (paragraph 7).

This increase in consciousness of a particular motif does not detract from involvement *because the original perception of it was spontaneous*. The increase in consciousness becomes coordinated with natural tastes, and this particular dialectic produces maximum subjective involvement, showing a periodic alternation between thoughts and feelings, response and deliberate thought. The increase in conscious action on M's part also accounts for her increasing use of the phrase "the reader" and her apparently customary reliance on phrases like "Lawrence says" or "Lawrence describes." But unlike L's essay, M's does not, in the development of her argument, use the assumptions on which such usages are based. The vestigial nature of these usages is much clearer in her essay.

Consider M's conclusion that "Because a word is important to *me*, it also is important to the story." This statement should be seen in terms of the original assignment, which was to write an argument on what "you think is the most important word in the story." The assignment appeared in that form in order to set the stage for discussion and to provide a familiar context for this new issue. Everyone thinks of the story as an object and no one thinks of it as an experience. But M's statement exhibits the logic of the primacy of subjectivity. The subjective importance is the first matter to be determined. Importance to the story is a result of importance to the reader. Thus, importance in the story is a secondary consideration. There is a new causal relationship set up. Literary importance is caused by subjective importance. It is a single process within which a critical judgment is always the result of a subjective response. Almost every critical discussion centers on which factors are the most influential in determining some sort of "objective" essence of a given work of literature. But here we see that such critical judgments are created not on the basis of "evidence," but on the basis of personal predilection and the ability to justify such predilection.

Example: The Teacher's Choice

I will now explore yet another judgment of the "most important word"—my own. I will include some of my own affective responses and associations so as to give a fairly full picture of what I mean by the "subjective action of a word."

"The Rocking-Horse Winner" has always been a favorite story of mine, and I get pleasure every time I reread it. I don't always like everything Lawrence writes, because sometimes his tendency to repeat things and words and phrases just gets the better of me and I get bored. Not so with this story, which seems to me to have just the right amount of everything I consider the best in Lawrence. By now, in my umpteenth reading, I respond to the repetition of the word "luck" with some humor and irony. Paul's inquiries about "luck" assume a mythical or eternal quality, filled with all kinds of subsidiary meaning. The statement at the end— "Mother, did I ever tell you? I am lucky"—especially stands out for me, believe it or not, for its subtlety and understatement. It connotes tremendous heroism for me, since the boy is lying in his death agony, yet remains true to his goal. The mother is unreachable, but the boy remains steadfast.

This persistence on the part of Paul, which I alluded to earlier as his "obsession," gives me pleasure in the many repetitions of the word "luck." Every time it is repeated, I feel it is one more heroic assault by the young boy on a transcendental dilemma. Paul somehow fears the impossibility of success yet believes in it nevertheless out of inward passion and faith. The verbal relentlessness of the single word builds inside me a growing sense of emotional relentlessness and activates my own values of personal persistence and stubborn refusal to give up. This particular value has a social root in my personality: it is part of what I think I have in common with my ancestors, the Jewish people. My communal identity is strengthened by this sense of persistence, as is my own self-esteem. I am reminded of my late father's remark at the death of his own father: "*Weiter*" [Further (we must go)] , he said on the morning after the funeral, determined to continue his own life in spite of his grief.

The very outset of the story is full of excitement for me: "There was a woman who was beautiful, who started with all the advantages, yet she had no luck." For God's sake, I immediately think, if she is so beautiful but is just not lucky, *I'll* be only too glad to supply the missing "luck." And so I am really hooked! Before I am even introduced to the hero, I assume his burden; with a kind of aggressive, perhaps adolescent bravado, I swallow the bait and plunge into the story. I soon discover that I have let myself in for a real spin, since this beautiful woman, for whom I just volunteered my services, "could not feel love." Fortunately, I can forget about her problem (consciously) and pay attention instead to the economic situation at home. My hero now comes into the picture, does some detective work, finds out exactly what luck is and how it is supposed to work, and finally tells his mother essentially what I told the beautiful woman: "Well, anyhow . . . I am a lucky person." I vaguely, but not prominently, remember that mother told Paul that the reason she is unlucky is that she married an unlucky husband—indeed, "very unlucky"—and because he is unlucky, she, mother, is therefore also unlucky. But no matter. What does matter is that I am a lucky person, and to prove it, I have a very lucky horse who can take me to the winner and really bring luck to the house.

When I think of "Paul and the Horse," I am reminded of my childhood record of "Peter and the Wolf." I remember the real fear I had of the wolf even as I was listening to the record and the musical narration. There was grandfather in the story, there was mother in the house, around somewhere, but father was not there. I am also reminded of how, at about the same age when I was ill, my mother would generously play cards with me, and let me win, just in order to make me feel better. I remember vividly to this day that strange anxiety and guilt I had when she did let me win. I felt that she should not have indulged me that way—even though I was only about seven at the time—and that the great satisfaction I had in the indulgence was countervailed by my irrational fear that it was somehow very wrong. So my feelings here reach a new level of complexity: Paul's winning horse, and my winning card, carry with them an unspoken freight of wrongdoing.

Again, no matter. Paul's winnings are as satisfying to me as they are to Paul, and my spirit of persistence helps me to back Paul completely. However, here a new thought occurs: Why is Paul keeping all this a secret? Why doesn't he just hand the money to his mother himself and really try openly to win her love? I am frustrated that all that persistence is not being put to the best use—according to my values, of course. Paul's mother thus begins worrying about him, as he becomes more frantic to win races. The anxieties of son and mother are parallel. Thus, the original and basic pleasure, signaled through the repetition of the word "luck," proceeds against a background of anxiety caused by the continued yet unspoken presence of a secret feeling.

My "most important word" exposes the anxiety and brings the pleasure to a climax in one stroke. The word is "Malabar," which Paul "screamed" out to his mother, as she in the climax of her anxiety "suddenly ... switched on the light, and saw her son, in his green pyjamas, madly surging on the rocking horse." The light "suddenly lit him up ... and lit her up, as she stood ... in her dress of pale green and crystal." The light is on in the house at last, I feel. It is on the son and on the mother. The son is in green and the mother is in green, and they are both caught by the suddenness of the mutual disclosure. Paul then triumphantly cries out the name of the winning horse twice. He then repeats the name obsessively and deliriously to Bassett. On the third day, Malabar wins and Paul is informed. And he then repeats Malabar's name hysterically six times to his mother as proof of his great luck. Paul "knew."

"Malabar" acts like a magic word. For the first time, Paul gives the word to his mother. Mother is informed of what Paul has been doing. My wish for that communication has been fulfilled. Paul's hitherto secret quest has become a public quest, and Paul shares his "knowledge" with his mother. In my association, my own malaise was due to the fact that I did not share with my mother my "knowledge" of what was wrong, but instead remained feeling guilty. Paul's knowing the right horse is like my knowing the "right" wolf, perhaps the missing support, guidance, or correction from father. Or, I feared that the "wolf" in my father would harm me for being alone with mother—and for taking advantage of her overindulgence. When Paul names the horse, he brings my unnamed fears to consciousness, and thus into control. He does it in a way especially suitable to my tastes and style: he screams out what he knows. I love to raise my voice, and I do, in reading these "Malabar" lines in class. I believe, in perhaps the most infantile of thoughts, that if I yell loud enough, someone will hear.

For me, the word here also represents knowledge. Paul says to Bassett, "I know!" and when the horse comes in, he says to his mother, "I knew Malabar, didn't I?" Paul, like any child, wants to know many things, especially about how things are between him, father, and mother. Paul especially wants to know that he is lucky, unlike his father. He wants to know that even if father doesn't have mother's love, he (Paul) does, and he wants to know this from his mother. So he tells her the magic word. He wants to know that love will conquer his anxiety. When Paul knows the magic word, I know what is behind my anxiety, and I realize the sources of my strong response to this story. I know why I feel guilt and anxiety, and I know that *telling* my mother how I feel will set things right. Knowledge for me means insight and self-control, so that saying the right word at the right time gives me pleasure in itself and allays my fears and anxieties.

My value of persistence has gained a victory. I had associated this value with my "ancestors," but particularly with my father and his way of coping with the death of his own father, a way which he taught to me. In a boy or young man there is a special guilt associated with the death of his father, namely, the suspicion that he has wished it all along. If one's own father can somehow allay this guilt, it is indeed a victory. Thus, the two aspects of my response go together: my father helped to allay my guilt, and I learned on my own, from the magic word, how to allay the same guilt through self-understanding—learning to say the right thing at the right time, as perhaps my father did when his father died.

Paul dies at the end of the story. To me, it is as if this event is not in the story. I see only the victory. But there is a reason even for this curious perception. To me, it is a Christian event and a religious necessity. Paul dies on the third day after his original knowledge. He is informed early by his mother that "Perhaps God" knows why "one person is lucky and another unlucky." Bassett is described as "serious as a church," and he repeatedly describes Paul's knowledge "as if he had it from heaven." To me, all of this religious material is unimportant and actually feels to me like an extraneous appendage to the story, though, intellectually, it all "fits." But the reason for my holding this opinion is that the religious material does not fit in with my "Jewish" value of persistence, which is emotionally activated in me by my reading. Self-sacrifice is an alien value and has always been repugnant to me. I simply do not respond to it, for it would ruin the whole train of pleasure I now gain from my reading. The truth is, I do not have it in me to respond to Paul's death: it somehow has nothing to do with what has taken place until his death. Essentially, what happens after Paul finds the magic word is irrelevant to me. My knowledge cannot kill me—it can only enhance my life. So, I part company with Paul after his victory, and even though I may understand what is happening for others reading the story, it remains emotionally alien to me.

By ordinary standards, this is a great deal to say about why a word is "most important in the story." But we are trying to enlarge ordinary standards, to show that one never speaks only about the story. Rather, we speak of the story only as it is a function of our reading experience. We are trying to enlarge our standards by understanding the subjective action of a word—or a passage or any other aspect of a work we may choose—and by understanding that a critical judgment follows right upon a subjective judgment of personal importance or emotional value. This value is discoverable through the techniques we have outlined in the previous section and that I have demonstrated in my discussion of this story. The subjective action of the word "Malabar," I think, is fairly clear from my discussion. But my critical judgment about the story is not clear.

The Connection between Response and Interpretation

Let me state my interpretation of the story and then try to show its connection with my emotional response. In a conventional critical context I would offer a psychological interpretation of the story. It is "about" a boy trying to "win" his mother's love by replacing in her life the "luck" which she claims her husband, the boy's father, cannot give her. He does this with a special magic rocking horse, which can bring riches when the boy "rides" him privately and intensely, even orgiastically. Then, by manipulating a few weak and greedy men around him—Bassett and Uncle Oscar—he gives the wealth to his mother in hopes that she will be satisfied enough to give him her love. When his mother learns of these efforts by walking in on his most hysterical effort yet, he dies in spite of his enormous success, begging his mother to recognize his special power. Psychologically, this means something like, "the wages of sin is death," that is, the penalty for gaining luck, which in this story is the special kind of power that the husband-father is supposed to have and doesn't, is death. If one actually fulfills the wish to replace father in mother's life, one must die. In the story, this replacement occurs at the climax, when the boy communicates his knowledge directly to his mother.

The most outstanding difference between the response and the interpretation is that the latter tries to include Paul's death in the logic of its argument. In my response, I simply dismissed Paul's death. It is tempting to argue that, since the interpretation is a conscious act guided by certain standards of completeness, I make the effort to include as many of the prominent events in the story as I can. But this would not be the correct reason for the difference. The fact is that Paul's death does play a part in my response, but *it is subjectively important that I ignore it.* Not only that, it is subjectively important that I lie about ignoring it and that I make believe that this ignorance plays an important part in my response. The reason for the lie is that I am trying to preserve a certain psychological pleasure, one not confined to the story, but one which exists on a permanent basis in my personality as a pleasure which the story stimulates every time I read it. Thus, in order to protect both the pleasure in my response and the sources of that pleasure in my personality, I hide the real nature of my response by adding into my interpretation something alien to my response, thus giving the interpretation a different character from the response. This new character is presented as apart from me, in its objective formulation: *Paul* has fulfilled a forbidden wish and so dies. This statement hides the nature of my own fears attendant upon entertaining the identical wish and also hides my very selective perception of the story. That is, it hides the entire subjective situation in me.

The "standard of completeness" is only the rationalization for the process I have just detailed. In critical interpretation it is simply not possible to be complete. How many aspects of this story have I omitted? How many elements of dialogue, of vocabulary, how many telling usages have I not noticed? Themes, such as gambling, I have not even mentioned? Many of my students say this story is about greed, and yet I barely mentioned this important human motive in connection with the story. How foolish, it seems to me, to pretend that completeness is a viable standard in criticism. No. The reasons for the shape and content of *both* my response and my interpretation are subjective. When my interpretation is viewed in the light of my response, it is abundantly clear that this is the case. If my interpretation were presented alone, however, we would be hard put to account for its characteristic shape, except if one wished to pigeonhole it as "Freudian." And even this label would tell little that would enable us to understand either my interpretation or our reading experience any better.

Framing the interpretive problem in terms of "importance,"

therefore, enlarges our critical perspective so that it may include the key influence of our emotional response. From a social point of view, this outlook does away with the priestly role critics have assigned themselves and renders their position of leadership far more resilient. Instead of being a self-appointed intermediary between the author and the reader, a critic can now claim to be just another reader, but one whose claims to authority rest on the forthright but systematic presentation of his own responsive capacities and tastes. When a critic or teacher says, "This is important, let us study it," his listeners may take what he says with the confidence that it is important to the critic and may or may not be important to anyone else. The whole activity of reading and literary involvement becomes an interpersonal affair with genuine give and take, and authority flows openly where it belongs—from the personal integrity and persuasive capacity of the critic-reader.

The Most Important Passage in "Her First Ball"

There is not much need, at this point, to discuss the process of selecting an important passage in the same detail that we considered the selection of the most important word. Let me then outline some of the different issues that arise in shifting the topic from the most important word to the most important passage—in this case, that of Katherine Mansfield's very short story, "Her First Ball."

The Story as a Report

In choosing the Lawrence story for the first class confrontation with the idea of importance, I obviously expect the majority to conclude what seems to be obvious—"The teacher wants us to write an essay on 'luck' in the story"—so that I may then start arguing with them about their choice, setting the stage for what I have to teach about importance. However, I conceive of the Mansfield story as having no really outstanding or obvious passage that one can easily choose as the most important—and there is no way that a student can guess that I am already thinking of a particular passage. I do expect in the ensuing essays, and I usually get, a good variety of passages. Consider first, briefly, the opening paragraph of one of my class's best "objectivist" critics:

> N. The most important passage in Katherine Mansfield's story "Her First Ball" is the following paragraph:
>
>> Leila gave a light little laugh, but she did not feel like laughing. Was it—could it all be true? It sounded terribly true. Was this

first ball only the beginning of her last ball after all? At that the music seemed to change; it sounded sad, sad; it rose upon a great sigh. Oh, how quickly things changed! Why didn't happiness last for ever? For ever wasn't a bit too long.

> The reason that this paragraph is the most important passage in the story is that for Leila, the main character, it represents a point of crisis; for it is at this point in the story that she is for the first time confronted with the necessity of choosing between two opposing courses of action regarding her enjoyment and acceptance of the ball; and, since the story can be taken to involve considerations of maturity and immaturity which in the universality of application transcend the mere acceptance or rejection of the ball on Leila's part, this passage can also be seen as the point at which she is forced for the first time to confront the less appealing aspects of her entrance into maturity.

N is clearly an experienced reader and can easily articulate the important generalities about works of literature. He thus singles out what he thinks is the main character's main source of conflict; the passage which finds this character at the crossroads of that conflict is the most important passage. N had heard my own thoughts about the Lawrence story and did an excellent job constructing the argument in this essay after the form of my argument about what I thought was the most important word in that first story. Thus, the passage he picked, and subsequently presented a very convincing argument for, shows the heroine at the point when the old man's words have touched her inwardly. I only point out that this kind of reasoning is again in terms of the story as a report of outside events, and N follows all the assumptions I enumerated when I discussed L's response to the Lawrence story. Essentially, N reasons about the story as if it were a piece of history, rather than something that intrinsically involved a subjective engagement. Good enough. In contrast, consider the response of O.

The Pretense of Critical Objectivity

1   O. No single passage in "Her First Ball" gave me a strong enough emotional or intellectual reaction to qualify the lines as "most important." My emotions were gradually built-up from the first paragraph on, then slowly, toward the end of the story, I got a slight intellectual response. Because of this, my reading experience was based on the story as a total unit, and not on any few isolated words or lines. Throughout the story I was impressed by three things: the pleasure of reading special figurative language, emotional responses gained by identifying with the character, and intellectual reflection. The emotional aspect was the most dominant of the three,

but I hesitate to say it was the most important. Instead, I propose that all three were integral parts in making the story successful.

2   The first metaphor of the story, "Perhaps her first real partner was the cab," was important because I reacted to it as beautiful figurative language. Standing alone—as it certainly does since it is the first paragraph—it adds little meaning to the story. At first I enjoyed it merely for its aesthetic value, but after finishing the story and returning to the beginning, I found that it actually made a comment on Leila's personality. She was young and idealistic and could change the atmosphere of her surroundings simply by changing her state of mind. She had created an inanimate object (the cab) into a dancing partner simply through her excitement and imagination. Now the paragraph had become important, but only when viewed as a part of the entire story. Alone it was great descriptive language, but that did not qualify it for "most important."

3   Another passage that was important in my total experience of the story is found on page 202 beginning, "He was tossed away on a great wave of music" and ending "sending them spinning." Again this gave satisfaction by being fine figurative language, and it enriched the story's value for me by giving insight into Leila's view of the ball itself. The music was soaring and dramatic, "a great wave," and the couples were not merely dancing but "spinning." This passage also provided an emotional release because it rid Leila (and me) of the little fat old man. Something bad was replaced with something beautiful, and I was very happy that the author had added those seemingly insignificant lines. However, since my actual reaction was only emotional, I don't feel this passage was the most significant.

4   One of my favorite groups of lines is the description of the ices on page 204. They are so "sweet" and frosty and "cold" and even the spoon was iced. Then comes the next sentence—the fat man is waiting for her at the door. What a contrast between the idealistic and reality! But these sentences were only effective because I quickly thought back to the first description of the fat old man— "bald," "murmuring" with a "black" program—where I discovered how distasteful he was.

5   A contrast between the different ways of viewing life seemed to be an important part of this story. Through Leila's eyes I saw the ball as brilliant and exciting. After reading how her cousins, her partners, the chaperones and the fat old man viewed the ball, I could see that life was merely a state of mind. This was an important message in the story, but it did not come from any single passage. Instead, a gradual accumulation of single events within the story lead to this conclusion. Because of this, four additional passages gained importance. The paragraph starting "Oh, dear, how hard it was to be *indifferent* like the others ... It even gave her a pang to see her cousin Laurie throw away the wisps of tissue ... she would have ... kept those wisps" gave the first clue that others were not

as enthralled with the dance as Leila. At the time I read it, it did not really strike me this way. I vaguely skipped over it, and it did not gain importance until I read that her partners were not too impressed either. Two passages were needed for this information: "the voice . . . sounded tired" continuing down to "Certainly her partner did not say very much," and another when her second partner again asked her if she liked the floor and "Perhaps it was a little strange that her partners were not more interested." Both these men are bored in contrast to her excitement, and after reading these passages I remembered her cousin's boredom. This is the point when I began to realize that the reason Leila found the ball so exciting was her attitude. Finally the fat man's description of the chaperones' view of the ball and ultimately *his* view of life itself showed that it definitely was up to the individual to make life into whatever he wanted. Here an important idea in the story required four passages to convey the thought.

6   Not until the last paragraph did I gain both an emotional and intellectual reaction to the story, plus the personal enjoyment of a descriptive metaphor. Slowly, through the description of the music, I could tell Leila would survive the fat man's horrible account of the future. The stars had acquired "wings." A "soft, melting . . . tune began," and "in one minute, in one turn, her feet glided, glided." Personally I enjoyed the language. Emotionally I was glad because Leila was glad. Intellectually I pieced the story together and discovered that Leila and the fat man enjoyed the ball because they *wanted* to. At first I thought this would be the most important paragraph, but standing alone it was nothing at all, aside from the word structure itself. It required all of the preceding experiences in the story to give it importance.

7   I have cited nine passages which together made me understand the story as a total unit. Taken separately, every passage had importance, but none was prominent enough to be called most important. Each passage gained significance through an interplay of all the words in the story. Each line added to the one preceding it until the conclusion, when a unified effect was accomplished.

I should record, before discussing the details of this response, that in the essay assignment sheet, I allowed that some might not believe there was such a thing as a "most important passage," and that those who held this view should try to reason out in their essays why they thought this was the case. O's essay took just this tack.

The important result of O's efforts for us is that her essay gives us a subjective account of a relatively familiar New Critical process of accumulating evidence for an argument. The development of the *sense* of importance is a cumulative process. N's argument above was actually developed in a manner quite similar to O's, but N presents the argument retrospectively, with the

proposition first and the evidence for it later. Subjectively, however, this does not happen, for in responding one does not want
or need to prove anything, though one does seek to develop a
sense of the reading experience. Only if one assumes there is
really such a thing as "the most important passage in the story,"
a passage that implicitly all *must* accept, can one offer an essay
in the proposition-proof format. Therefore, when O challenges
the implied assumption of the essay assignment, the result is a
subjective account. The explanation of the challenge she presents
in the first paragraph details three different factors, all of which
are subjective: "the pleasure of reading special figurative language, emotional responses gained by identification with the
character, and intellectual reflection." Even the latter factor,
which is most usually transformed into critical judgments, is
patently a subjective process: no claim is made that intellectual
reflection, which includes ratiocination, deduction, inference,
and so on, leads to results any more binding on others than do
the first two subjective processes.

In paragraph 2, O actually names the process I had claimed was
covertly operating in N's response. Referring to the cab as being
Leila's first partner, O reports, "At first I enjoyed it merely for
its aesthetic value, but after finishing the story and returning
to the beginning, I found that it actually made a comment on
Leila's personality." You will observe, I am sure, O's objective
language here: "it" made a comment. But it is not hard to see,
in spite of this language, that the first metaphor O noticed acted
on her *conception* of Leila. O reported that she identified with
the heroine, and there can be little doubt that what O calls "aesthetic" pleasure acts subjectively insofar as it enhances the
process of identification, i.e., "I was so eager (vicariously) for
a partner, and partners seemed more and more important as I
continued reading, that when I reviewed the partnership of the
cab, it seemed to underscore a sense of importance I had gradually
been developing." This cumulative nature of the reading experience acts out in miniature the cumulative nature of all subjective
experience. The familiar "aha" experience we all have as we see
a new event in the light of past history is due to a fundamental
natural tendency to perceive experience automatically in the
light of (usually) unconsciously established patterns of perception.

The observation concluding paragraph 3 is unique in the response because of its negative tone. Since O's response to the
lines was "only emotional," she denies that the passage was most
significant. This is an excellent example, even in this unusually
subjective account, of the natural resistance most people have

to give major credit to something that is "only emotional." O's main point in this essay shows that this is the case: the passage and the response were probably more important to her than she claims. In paragraphs 5 and 6, O issues her central judgments: "the reason Leila found the ball so exciting was her attitude" (5), "I . . . discovered that Leila and the fat man enjoyed the ball because they *wanted* to" (6), and "I could see that life was merely a state of mind" (5). In the middle of paragraph 3, O states that the passage which evoked the "[merely] emotional" reaction "enriched the story's value for me by giving insight into Leila's view of the ball itself." In light of O's central judgments, her disclaimer at the end of paragraph 3 involves a contradiction, for O discovers that Leila's subjective view of the ball—indeed the views of all the characters—was the most important idea for her. Just as O's response to this passage was "only emotional," Leila's view of the ball was "only" subjective. Even in O's essay, the need for an intellectual act is consciously still more important than other needs. O phrases her main idea as a discovery about the story, rather than about her response. Yet, the most important pleasure she takes from the story is that she develops, through her identification with Leila, the sense that it is a state of mind, an attitude, an ability to enjoy because one wants to enjoy, which is the most important source of emotional satisfaction for the heroine, and implicitly, for herself. O actually unconsciously translated an unconscious feeling—pleasure in the subjective development of one's own pleasure—into conscious terms and made it the thesis of her essay. Only as a thesis *about the story* did O present her discovery about the primacy of subjectivity, when all along this was operating in her reading and responsive experiences. To me, this is a remarkable demonstration of how deeply ingrained it is, even in those most willing to explore their responses, to diminish the importance of "purely" emotional reactions.

In this light, O's original thesis regarding the cumulative nature of the sense of importance is really of secondary importance in her essay, though it obviously remains a fundamental fact about response. This original thesis now can be seen as a very subtle disguise for the major accomplishment of the essay: O's triumphant identification with the heroine, which gave her renewed confidence in her own subjectivity—her attitude, state of mind—as well as her "insight" into "the story." From a subjective standpoint, there really is a "most important passage" for O. She says, after pointing to the passage where Leila resolves to reenter the ball and is taken over by a dancing partner, "At first I thought this would be the most important paragraph..." but then adds, "standing alone it was nothing at all." But O never did read this passage "standing alone." She read it only in the right sequence, and she experienced the major intuition that this was the "most important" passage to her since everything came together *in her mind* through its stimulus. But then, the need for an intellectual thesis created an intervening idea that was untrue to her response, namely, that the passage somehow stood "alone." No passage ever stands alone, even if one is an objectivist critic. But the emotional need to diminish the recognition of the primacy of subjectivity created in O this intellectual disturbance and brought her back to what we may call the "frame" thesis of the essay—no one passage is most important.

There is something important in common between O's frame thesis and my own interpretive remarks about the Lawrence story. Both exhibit a kind of dishonesty in relation to the response from which they were derived. The true scope of feeling—or perhaps the true limitations of feeling—is essentially denied by intellectual reformulations. It is not all that clear why they should undergo such a transformation. But it is clear that there is a systematic connection between the emotional response materials and the intellectual reformulations.

The first and easiest solution to this problem has a strong claim on our belief: that is, emotional responses are not held in common, but the *text* of the story is—two people may easily agree on the "itness" of the story. Therefore, an intellectual statement is framed on the assumption of such a mutual agreement. It would thus seem that there is a benevolent social purpose to objectivist studies of literature—the attempt to state what as many readers as possible have in common. Perhaps in many cases this is exactly the purpose, but it is never the only purpose: only in exceedingly few instances do objectivist interpretations receive general acceptance. Therefore, neither the emotional response *nor* the interpretations are actually held in common on a large scale. We are driven to the alternative solution, namely, that it is subjectively important to *pretend* that there is a common ground—to present our thoughts as if there were. This accomplishes two things. First, it allows us to think of ourselves as contributing members of a certain community, builders of the common intellectual storehouse of "knowledge." Second, it protects what is supremely important to us in a psychological sense: our private feelings, our narcissistic predilections, fetishes, hangups, fixations, and other unconscious emotional schemata over which we have next to no control. Since we don't control them, we disguise them— act as if they play a small part in our lives. However, our present understanding of the key role of subjectivity does not do away with the social goal of interpretive work. Rather it gives this goal new authority and binding power, while reducing its pretended scope to more realistic size.

We will discuss this problem further in the next chapter, but let us now consider what is involved in the third phase of my procedure, choosing the most important aspect of the work of literature, whatever that aspect may turn out to be.

The Most Important Aspect of "The Turn of the Screw": The Teacher's Choice Again

The option to choose which aspect of a work of literature to discuss as being "most important" gives us an opportunity to explore the logic of my suggested sequence. I suggested earlier that there is no imperative to move in the sequence *word, passage,* and *aspect in general.* While I still hold to this principle, it might be of some interest to explain what my experience in this regard has turned up. This last question— what is the "most important" aspect— is an open-ended one: there is no easy way to see what kind of answer will do. Only to those students who have been exposed to traditional New-Critical concepts of literary study will this question begin to have meaning. While there are no stable definitions of such things as plot, character, figurative language, comedy, and so on, an experienced student will know roughly what they are, and, in a pinch such as this, will try to apply them to the problem at hand. He might say, for example, that the *story* is the most important feature of "The Turn of the Screw," and he will go ahead and present an objectivist argument. Moreover, it is likely that such students will select their aspects from this traditional list. In the subsequent discussion of these essays, it will be difficult to avoid discussing how to define the categories, with the result that the question of importance is pushed into the background.

To a student who is not aware of these rough categories, the problem is especially confusing. This is not so much because he has to think out the question carefully and ask about what he doesn't understand, but more because this whole process of intellectual assault on an unfamiliar problem creates anxiety that will intrude upon the person's spontaneous sense of importance or subjective value. I am assuming this method to be presented in an introductory context. One of our primary aims is to reduce or even eliminate the normal diffidence most students have about intellectual or academic enterprises. We would like to show dramatically that schoolwork is not abstract and distant, or that it requires a fund of complex information, but that it is an activity which proceeds from the most common and familiar aspects of daily life. It is therefore much more reassuring to most students to delay the application of traditional intellectual categories until the emotional groundwork has been laid.

The choice of the most important aspect, finally, requires two different decisions. To make these decisions, one must already be in the habit of observing one's response. The first awareness, the one we have been discussing mainly thus far, is of the fact of one's own involvement: one has to stop for a moment and ask oneself, Why do I want to get to the next page? or, Why do I like or dislike being in the world of this particular work? The second question is, Can I name any palpable textual regularity that especially promotes my response? Now it may or may not be true that a word is a simpler textual regularity than an image pattern or habitual usage, but it is not the intrinsic complexity of the aspect that is at issue. It is simply that a word has much more in common with the experience of everyday life than an image pattern, though most people can identify the latter if it is explained in enough detail. By the time someone has thought about a number of his responses, the everyday meaning of things like image patterns, or particular sorts of interpersonal confrontations, will have become clear. A person will already understand the term "aspect" or "feature" in the same everyday sense that he understands "word" — as an element of subjective experience in general, not just literature. The whole series of "literary" categories will lose its preemptive hold on the possibilities for response. The response will therefore be able to *define its own categories,* some of which may after all be part of the traditional list. The new categories will be much more likely to be representatives of the reader's taste and perceptual style, and writing about literature will be much more visibly connected with the reader's own special interests.

Let me briefly discuss, then, some of the possibilities Henry James's "The Turn of the Screw" offers for choosing an important aspect. In my experience this tale has never failed to work up the imaginations of readers. The levels of response and thought that consistently appear rival the response levels of Shakespeare's and Dostoevski's great works. Unlike these works, moreover, its language and train of thought are relatively simple, at least on first readings!

The most important aspect of "the story" for me is the same

reason I think it is especially suitable for presenting this problem in class. Probably not coincidentally, this same aspect has had a lively critical history since Edmund Wilson stirred up the dust a few decades ago. In the critical literature the question is whether or not the governess is telling "the truth." Subjectively put, the question becomes, Do I believe in this narrator, and can I identify with her, and why do I feel this way? This question returns us to the first issue we considered in this section—that literature becomes recognizable as such by an act of mind of the reader. With a slight variation, this initial subjective act becomes the object of my attention in reading this story. I will not elaborate about my way of handling this response, but I will indicate that I do it by concentrating on what I can find out about the mind of the *author*, and by what I can put together from Leon Edel's biography of Henry James regarding the relationship of the author to this story.

The basic subjective question is of special interest in class, I have found, because few readers are bored with the story, whether they believe the governess's narration or not. Somehow, the reading experience is not interfered with, and is almost always intensified by, the question of the governess's veracity. Also, although the majority of students do come to suspect the narrator, there are always a significant number who take her at her word, and who are, pell mell, terrified by the ghosts. The subjective problem to be explored, therefore, is whether there is anything in *common* in the responses of those who believed and those who did not. This is not an easy question to pursue, and this is a case where examination of affects and associations will come in very handy. However, I will discuss my own subjective reaction, and then only to suggest what might be held in common, and thus what might be "important" about this aspect of the tale.

In discussing my own affective reaction, I will take advantage of a feature of my relationship to this work that is not held in common with that of most students but which probably *is* held in common with that of most other teachers. That is, my affective response to the work has changed since my first contact with the work. In early readings, I believed the narrator, while in later readings, primed by the critical arguments and the study of James's biography, my response to the work became increasingly complex and interested, to the point where I began taking various kinds of initiative to make my sphere of interest ever larger—reading further criticism, teaching the work in various contexts to various classes, discussing with colleagues their responses, among other things. It is this elaborateness of the reading experience, for most of the works confronted in class, which represents a teacher's authority. I think it is clear that this authority carries its own weight of respectability and that it defines in extensive and detailed terms how a teacher is different from a student, and what it is the teacher has to teach. I mentioned earlier that the difference between teacher and student is that the teacher has lived longer and has a greater familiarity with what he is teaching. This difference would be a rather commonplace matter, unworthy of special notice, were it not for the fact that it comes into play pragmatically in the discussion and exploration of response. The teacher has a "before-and-after" experience, he has a long memory of how his interest developed, and he therefore can report how his feelings for a work changed in accordance with his own growth. As I think back over my own college and graduate school days, I can remember the "teacher's yellowed notes" experience that so many students complain about now. The student's disappointment is not simply that the teacher is using the same notes he used twenty years ago, or even five years ago: perhaps those notes are worthwhile hearing from again. Rather, it is the suspicion that the literary work in question is no longer really living within the teacher any more, that it is not a subject of his current thoughts. The subjective logic of emulation then tells me that if the teacher does not think this work is important to him now, why should it be important to the student? Even in graduate school, the process of learning is still through emulation rather than instruction: the students' conceptions and feelings about the teacher have the most telling effect on the process of learning. I have set out this principle in some detail in an essay I wrote some years ago, "Psychological Bases of Learning from Literature."* Any student who cares about his schoolwork is importantly involved with the personality of the teacher, even if in a less than fully conscious way. The teacher takes advantage of this involvement by citing his own history of response, thereby making very clear how he is like the student and how he is different. In observing this demonstration the student does precisely the same thing: he sees how he is the same and how he is different from the teacher, thus creating for himself a new identity element and validating the entire learning experience.

It is in this spirit, therefore, that I report my responses to "The Turn of the Screw." I speak now as a teacher, whereas, in re-

---

College English 33 (October 1971): 32-45.

sponse to the Lawrence tale, I spoke as another responding member of the class.

In my first readings of the tale, I was not very impressed. I had a mild interest in the outcome. Probably the most important aspect of the story for me was the two children, how they seemed to be terrorizing the governess, and how peculiar it was that they ended up terrorized, and in Miles's case, dead. My feelings, I judge, were ordinary and not too strong. The most authentic feeling I did have was that the two children were extremely precocious and somewhat too powerful for just children. (For subjective reasons which my associations would reveal, I have an eye for powerful children.) My view of the governess was that she was a rather weak and strange figure, but it never did enter my head that her report might not be "reliable" in the ordinary sense. To a large extent, this view of the governess obtains among the "naive" readers in my classes now: some get more pleasure, some less than I did, but that is essentially the feeling of such readers.

My relationship to this tale began to change under the influence of someone who turned out to be a very important teacher in my life, Leon Edel, in whose course I read the tale for the first time. His classroom manner was almost too nonchalant to attract my notice, but there was no mistaking his pleasure in asking the class for the name of the narrator. He asked other questions like this, and he always looked like the cat who ate the canary as he awaited a response. It soon emerged that neither the governess nor the original narrator were named, and the teacher's pleasure in asking such questions became a matter of significant interest for me. Edel's own relish in posing the problem was the instigating experience in my developing interest. The upshot was, simply, that I made his pleasure my pleasure, and then developed it in my own way.

My perceptual shift may be explained rather simply as a turn from an interest in the children to a much more intense interest in the governess and in the technique of narration. The change in my affect was from simple feelings to extremely complex ones. The emotional process of developing trust in the narrator was accompanied by an intellectual curiosity about the "facts" of the narration, and these two issues combined in the feeling, What does the governess really want? Let us observe this feeling from a slightly different angle. The governess is an attractive young woman to whom I am constrained to listen. Her story (to me) is confidently told, yet marked by a constant underlying protest of her innocence. I am in her power, yet I wonder if I trust her. The children, whose power was originally impressive to me, are also in terror of her and, as I slowly conclude, are likewise in the power of her narration. I am also impressed by her ability to present conversations which seem conclusive but which leave enough unsaid to make me suspect her veracity. Therefore, the question of my feelings becomes, What is my relationship to this woman? — and that question is the "most important aspect" of my reading experience.

Soon, the question of the reality of the ghosts becomes unimportant to me. I read the criticism and learn that but for one passage, the ghosts seem assuredly to be a creation of the governess's imagination. I ignore that passage, for I am fascinated by the thought that the whole story is a creation of the governess's mind. For me, the governess becomes a psychological case, and I begin pondering the possible motives of the governess for telling such a tale. We may note that in my thinking in this way, I have taken the governess from "in here" and made believe she is "out there," a case, and not a function of my own subjectivity. Nevertheless, it remains true that my relationship to this woman is the central issue of my response.

I further discover that in spite of my attachment to her, the governess is rather removed from me. The tale opens with a narrator reporting that a group was out in the country in the winter telling ghost stories. One member of the group, Douglas, wanted to give the traditionally scary formula of a frightened child another "turn of the screw" by contributing a tale about two children. He had gotten the tale from his own former governess, now dead, but written, apparently, in her hand. We then learn that Douglas is now also dead and that the present narrator has the manuscript. He does not read the tale from the manuscript, but reports on Douglas's reading of the tale that night some days after Christmas. My feeling with regard to all these maneuvers is that I can't quite tell if the narrator is a man or a woman, or if the tale is being presented to me in the present or in the past, or if the narrator is one of the living or the dead. I am annoyed at all of this confusion, because now I know even less about my relationship with the narrator or governess or author, or, finally, James himself.

My interest in the governess is even more complicated by the kinds of things that attract my attention the most in the story— questions of love and sex. I am told early that the governess was in love, and I am left to assume that she was in love with the man who hired her. She becomes terrified by two ghosts who, we vaguely suspect, may have been involved with one another, or perhaps they were both involved with the boy Miles, or perhaps just Peter Quint was involved with Miles. Peter Quint, whose name for me calls attention to both male and female genitals (Peter, a slang word for penis, and quint, from the Chaucerian "Quainte" for cunt), is seen by the governess either from the waist up only, or as a shadow in the dark. The governess herself is obviously involved with Miles, and her attachment to him seems to smother him. Miles would prefer to go back with the boys. Therefore, in addition to the other confusions, there is an unnamable sexual element in my interest in the governess. Finally, Miles, who I perceive emotionally as my ·rival for the governess's attention, dies at the end, but even so I don't know where I am, since the governess seems to be possessed by yet another man—the image or spirit or person Peter Quint himself.

The upshot of all of these feelings is that I am tremendously involved with a powerful, sexual woman who does not admit her sexuality to me and who seems to me to either kill men or become irrationally possessed by them. My situation with regard to the governess, it turns out, is more familiar in real life than it might seem, since it represents the feelings of the oedipal child toward his mother, conscious of her sexuality yet confused by it, seeing her as "possessed" by another man yet having an overwhelming power over babies or small children. Sexual matters are not yet really clear, but there is a distinct consciousness of sexual differences without the actual knowledge of how they work.

For me, this is the key: *without the actual knowledge.* I complained about this problem in various forms in the preceding paragraphs. But what is my solution? Earlier, I indicated two important factors about the history of my relationship to this tale: first, that my response to it became interesting to me under the influence of my teacher, Leon Edel, and second, that my preferred solution to the mystery of the story is biographical. Clearly, there is an important connection between these two facts, since Edel is the major biographer of Henry James, the author. The connection is that my solution involves my identifying with Edel, first, and then with James, two real men instead of one mysterious woman.

Edel, an older man, the same age as my late father and who in many ways evokes a similar response in me, was *my first source of enlightenment* about the story. He enlightened me by telling that the governess has *no* name. By itself this fact might be enlightening, but what made me pay important attention to it was the pleasure Edel took in announcing the fact. Because of Edel's patent enthusiasm, I emulated him and also became enthusiastic about the very same fact. My enthusiasm and its pleasant association with a father-type teacher motivated my independent interest in a whole new train of thought and response. The lack of identity in the governess, interestingly, leads to a positive identification of my interest in her because of the association of this new fact with an important teacher.

In finding my own solution, these initial conditions carry me even further. I emulate Edel once more and become an apprentice biographer. I rely on Edel's exhaustive detective work on James, and ferret out from this work the material I need to solve the mystery of this tale. I should add that Edel's discussion of the work is not satisfactory for me. Instead I put together his facts in a different way in order to create my own solution, and thus I create a new identity element or piece of self-knowledge from the inheritance of my teacher.

Edel's discussion identifies Miles with James. This is unsatisfactory to me for a number of reasons. The first reason is that I must understand my response to the governess; my feelings about Miles are not at all as strong. The second reason has to do with an intellectual rule of thumb I have had for a long time about literature. The author of a work of literature, I intuit, is always most fully identifiable with his hero, regardless of the gender of either. (Let us not argue about this principle, for its present importance is only that I ascribe to it.) This rule allows me to transform the mysterious woman into an identifiable man. With this translation in mind, all the other narrators are also the author, and I now understand why the original narrator had told Doublas that he had a title, which is the title by which we know the story, even if Douglas did not. My reconstruction of the story is based on James's habit of seeing himself as an innocent woman instead of a mature man. James disguises the masculine power he really does have by presenting it in the form of a woman with, in this case, an extraordinary and perhaps pathological imagination, or in the more common instances, with an exceptionally refined consciousness. Edel points out that James "killed off" Miles because, as a child, it was emotionally unsafe for the young Henry to exercise his real little-boy feelings, though it was not unsafe to exercise such feelings in the guise of the governess.

In my solution, I am myself neither a little boy chasing a mysterious sexual woman, nor am I identified with her, though both of these feelings were present at some point in my response. Mine is the usual oedipal solution, where the boy *identifies* with father in order to gain a mental correlative for the power he sees and perhaps fears in the father. This identification also helps overcome the poorly managed sexual feelings stimulated in me by my reading. If I adopt a fatherly stance, I may permit myself such feelings without fear since this stance improves the poor management. The fear I get from both children and governess is replaced by knowledge. Indeed, in this context, the governess's fear of Quint is the young boy James's fear of the mysterious strength of his father and brother.

I have thus gained the missing knowledge: I now know who the governess is. The full extent of my relationship with the governess has been exposed. I first identify with Miles as a strong little boy; I then replace this identification by an identification with the governess. The ambivalent feelings I have about this identification become wishes to *know* more about *her,* thus projecting her out of me and containing my sexual feelings. Finally, I translate my identification with her into an identification with Edel and James, and everything is under control. I now know what I didn't know before. The history of my relationship with this story shows that I have transformed myself from a naughty boy into a knowledgeable man, through identification with my teacher.

As a teacher, therefore, I have taken advantage of two different responses of mine in order to explore two different instances of what might be considered important aspects of this tale— a child's fear and a man's sexual interest and resulting search for (carnal?) knowledge. In exercising my small authority as a teacher, I related one of my own experiences with my teacher. What I as a teacher see is in terms of my own experiences of teachers. I related one of the ways in which I was helped along to become a teacher. Obviously, the aspects people will pull out are without limit. In terms of the *kinds* of things people selectively see, many other choices were demonstrated in our discussions of other response to other words. In choosing a special aspect, I think, a student has to have developed a history of emotional response, however brief. He has to be able to "become" his own teacher in order to make this more complex observation of his response. One has to have given oneself the luxury of responding freely, and also taken the additional responsibility of understanding that response. This small identity element (the awareness of one's own response) provides the necessary emotional preparation to undertake a more complex exploration of one's own response.

This kind of exploration sets the stage for our next large step— understanding interpretation as a communal act. Pragmatically, this means developing an ability to learn from one's peers and to see one's own knowledge as a sharable item. In normal development, a child does not begin learning from and in a group until he has learned to learn from his parents and family. That is why he begins school at four or five years of age. Analogously, in the present process, dealing with subjective experiences in a community should be preceded by the student's working things out on an individual basis, usually with the teacher and himself alone. Only now, therefore, may we try to understand subjective interpretation as a communal—or class—activity.

Interpretation as a Communal Act

Introduction: What "Others" Think

In proposing this method, I am often told that my attention to how people feel when they read is inimical to the efforts of the critical community to discover new knowledge about literature. In response to such criticism, I claim that just the opposite is the case. By working with the emotional responses of critics and readers, the authority of the community is enhanced rather than diminished, and abundant new knowledge about literary experience is made available. The traditional interpretive knowledge, furthermore, far from being rejected, is prominently retained — as anyone can tell from my own discussions above — and placed in a much more general and intellectually reliable context. This context is even more systematic and internally consistent than any set of critical standards heretofore invoked. But most important, the new context addresses itself to matters that are most germane to any reader, but which have previously been excluded from study for reasons that are ultimately detrimental to literary study. These matters are the personality and taste of the individual reader, and the primary need of any community for a fund of common knowledge, experience, and belief.

We confront at this point this second issue: How does one make use of the subjective responses of others, and how much of such responses are common on a larger scale — in a class, in a certain age-group, in a society, and so on? In my discussion of the James tale, you can probably discern the beginnings of my viewpoint. That is, we have a response to other people's opinions or feelings to the extent that we respond to the other people as individuals. We respond to nuances in their voice and manner, and to our own unconscious perception of the emotional backdrop of their view. But this much I have already demonstrated. If we take the matter further, the question becomes, How do feelings and values held in common by a group make their effect known in response, and how do people perceive group values in other people's responses?

This is probably the most difficult question we have yet confronted. Even in professional psychological circles there is considerable uncertainty about how individuals function in groups. Yet we cannot avoid this issue, first, because our interest as teachers is after all in a very special yet altogether familiar group — the collection of students in a class — and second, because values held in common always have a special place in our distinctive repertoire of emotional possibilities. That is, it makes a very big difference to us to know that others think and feel the way we do. This universal wish to validate at least some of our own feelings by discovering them in others is at the root of the collective establishment of values. These unnamed "others" could represent various groups — people in the same classroom, of the same sex, same age, same marital status, and so on. In exploring this problem, I would like to examine a group of responses to Thackeray's *Vanity Fair* and then try to pick out the group values on a few different levels. That is, I would like to see if we can observe certain values automatically assumed by members of a group to be jointly held by many others, and if so, observe how these values play a role in determining the character of the responses. Subsequently, I would like to see to what extent a group of class responses has a character of its own — How does this *class* feel about this novel?

I realize that it is not an easy matter to collect and analyze material from every single member of a class. Yet there is no alternative to doing this. In order to understand a group one must have material from each member of that group. In so many classes, under present customs, essays are assigned weekly or biweekly. They are quickly graded or evaluated, returned, and the class moves on to the next project. A teacher may therefore want to make fewer assignments, spending more time on each one. Or assignments might be given to only half the class at once, while the other half acts as observers and critics. In large classes this method is impossible; one can attempt it only in groups of not much more than thirty. Nevertheless, there is no avoiding the need to work with the group as a whole, assembling the contributions of each member and viewing them in aggregate.

Finally, I know of no student who is not tremendously eager to know what everyone else is thinking about and who will not jump at the opportunity to compare his own work with that of others, even if he will do this only in private, without admitting his own curiosity. Analysis of each person's work is here substituted for grading it. The arbitrary element of a teacher's authority is eliminated and only his analytical guidance is retained. In activities such as this, a student's natural sense of his own authority is given fullest play.

Consider, then, the following group of partially edited and abridged responses to Thackeray's *Vanity Fair*.

Responses to *Vanity Fair*

P. ...an extra aura of mystery due to the incongruency of the denotations of the words vanity and fair. ... Becky argued with Miss Pinkerton and eventually threw her dictionary out of the coach window. ... Here I became very close to Mr. Thackeray and his novel. ... I became immediately attached to William Dobbin, first out of a kind of pity and then out of respect. ... This is the type of sensitive yet strong man that every girl dreams of marrying some day. ...[The author's intrusions comprise] the one major point that struck me as being "Victorian." I kept wishing that Thackeray had not found it necessary to expostulate on his own views and the ways of the world all of the time. ...

Q. Amelia and Becky are both bound into the Victorian Code for Women, and neither one of them questions it....I lost patience with this weak-willed and clinging woman [Amelia] who let every chance of Fate knock her over....I found it quite a delight to watch how [Becky] played on the feelings of others, claiming from them on the basis of the Code treatment which she in no way honestly deserved. ... Amelia ... could not exist outside her century, while Becky Sharp could, and does, exist in every time. ... I must feel admiration for a Becky Sharp....Yet were such a woman to come in contact with me, I would detest her. For she would be doing what I would wish to do, but doing it better and ... successfully. ... The distinctly and exclusively Victorian heroine comes out with ... peace and prosperity in a Victorian hothouse.

R. It was the continual rigidity—like being suspended in a sexual climax—that dragged me down and made it so hard for me to read the novel. ...Thackeray seems to be building up to a sexual crescendo ... but he affords his reader no "release." ... The lack of any sexual scene whatsoever ... is parallel to the lack of sexual release—the effect, especially in my case, is a "tense" reader....a woman can function perfectly during coitus without ever achieving a climax. Herein lies one of the great problems of the book—it is typically "female" oriented. It is this, I believe, that makes it a "Victorian" novel. . . . To the modern reader, at least to me, "getting a booth in Vanity Fair" is no substitute for getting "a piece of ass." . . . female dominance . . . exemplified itself in the secretiveness of the book. Everyone . . . is always trying to get someone else's money or inheritance, or friendship or husband—without them noticing it . . . this sly secretiveness seems to be totally feminine to me. And I don't like it. . . . Thackeray *is* Vanity Fair, and if you don't like the author as a person, which I didn't, you simply can't like the book. He seems to have no moral vision. . . . He made me sick . . . he kept butting in and "putting in his two-cents worth" every chance he got. . . . I pictured Thackeray himself as very feminine . . . I could just see the wimp now, sitting primly at his desk, with a gorgeous plumed pen, dainty lace cuffs, and a pretty little silver teacup at his wrist. (You ought to get out with the boys more, Willie.)

S.   *Vanity Fair* makes me sick. . . . Perhaps . . . my feeling of nausea is due to the money quibbling, social climbing, simpering, effeminate, wasteful, ostentatious, phoney, mercenary, hypocritical tableaus and character in every booth at *Vanity Fair.* . . . Thackeray himself does not escape my mocking laughter. . . . I can only vomit at the characterization of our wealthy old maid Miss Crawley. . . . Thackeray repeats his sermons on Sammyism . . . till I am about to puke. . . . [Amelia] is just as revolting as her fat feminine brother Jos. . . . [Becky] is rotten and I admire her for it. . . . She too is after money . . . but at least she has brains, is honest to herself, and best of all, she has fun. . . . But Thackeray makes her even worse . . . all her antics add up to zero. Poo on him she is MY heroine. . . . The men are women and the women are nothing. They aren't even sexy. . . . These things are difficult medicines to swallow.

T.   I was quite enthralled with the story at first, and I enjoyed the style of writing, as it reminds me of books I enjoyed as a child. [*Little Women, Black Beauty, Jo's Boys*] . . . I enjoyed Thackeray's pompous air of British righteousness. . . . This avoidance of sex technique became annoying, simply because he seemed deliberately to be ignoring a fact . . . I resent this omission . . . I greatly enjoy his dialogue. . . . I also enjoy [his] general comment on the qualities of women in this very womanesque novel. I did not enjoy the emasculation [sic] of men . . . people who disappear after dinner to smoke *far* from the ladies . . . Thackeray is *not* impressing me with this worldly use of fashionable French. . . . And yet [he] has the nerve to say "They talked in English, not in bad French, as they do in the novels"! . . . there is no honesty in the relationship [between Amelia and Dobbin]—it is built on rules of courtship and modesty, and not at all on the mutual sincerity I find so important in the "true love" the Victorians looked for as much as I do.

U.   The characters are dull and depthless. . . . They seem to hide their true emotions on every matter from sex to war and every action that might prove exciting. . . . I am disturbed and impatient with Thackeray as he substitutes words into the place of emotional reaction and after inciting an initial response, he fearfully fails to carry through. . . . I have to conclude that there is a fear of honest expression, and the massive bulk of the book does a good job of suppressing emotional responses. . . . we see the true character of Becky and we react to her with some admiration for her spunk and her own fiery emotional responses. [Everyone else is] carefully dressed up in mounds of flaccid verbiage.

V. . . . absolute drudgery . . . during this gigantic chronicle in which love affairs play a very important part, there was not one good sex scene. . . . I confess that I have lowered myself many times to the sordid level of reading "dirty books" . . . love is very much lacking because it is unimportant in most of the characters' lives, it takes a lower position on the scale of meaningful things in life. . . . the people in the story don't really do a damn thing . . . God, do the women sing so damn much in this novel! . . . he deserves all the credit he gets for being a great author, but I'm afraid most of the activity in the book didn't interest me. . . . [Amelia] is so dependent upon people and so frail. . . . that's exactly the life I have lived; very sheltered and dependent upon my parents. But she is one of the few characters that is capable of any kind of love. . . . Actually her love sometimes got on my nerves. . . . In the end I saw her as a rather ridiculous sort of character; almost a child, she was so tender . . . but I had to admire her for her decency and sympathize with her struggles. . . . Most of the time I hated Becky . . . there was still some admiration underneath this antipathy. She seemed much more sensual to me . . . a fun-loving woman who enjoyed the presence of unorthodox lower-class people. . . .

W. . . . an enjoyable book for me to read . . . a chatty, rather gossipy story told by an interesting man who constantly throws out his ideas on what is going on in the story. The atmosphere is relaxed and untense. . . . Thackeray seems like a guide on a tour . . . an expert guide to us readers. . . . It was as if I was more of a spectator observing the characters and story, and not a person "living" the story. . . . The story didn't seem true-to-life to me . . . the lack of swear words. . . . The author's intrusions formed a good part of the story and . . . [they] would amuse and amaze me. Amuse me because they were often sarcastically funny, and amaze me for I would often think the very same thing before I read what he wrote.

X. [The author's] commentaries kept me from throwing the book down and giving the whole mess up to the wind . . . I began reading about a girls' school, the existence of which makes me furious. . . . After all, the large majority of a girl's life is the men she will become acquainted with . . . I believe in the role of woman as a wife and mother. Now that I have that out of my system, I can proceed with my more concrete emotions involved with the book. . . . My only interest in the novel was the commentary. . . . It is like thinking about something, never being able to find the words to describe my thoughts, and, then—pow! someone else has them all there in black and white. I think it's groovy! . . . I could grasp a bit of myself in Thackeray's injected statements. . . . I consider myself to be some-what of an expert on women, so I guess I liked what commentaries there were on this topic. . . . I was a bit more sentimental when I read the portions in the novel concerning the love of a mother for her children. . . . I liked the women. . . . They were interested in more of the same things that most well-bred women are, such as children, husbands, and a good life. . . .

Y. Aside from the overwhelming sense of nausea, my emotional responses . . . were very few and far between. . . . One aspect of the novel that tended consistently to amuse me was the brilliant, and very real, description of the characters. . . . [these characters] com-pensate for the breaks in consciousness the reader suffers at the expense of the author's intrusions . . . [further responses] were also elicited by the extreme prudence the author used in handling obviously racy aspects of the character's lives. [At one point] Thack-eray cuts in, arousing my curiosity: "Her sensibilities were so weak and tremulous, that perhaps they ought not to be talked about in a book." . . . [also], without the intrusion, a wonderment of Becky's private life (particularly her sex life) is created by . . . subtle sugges-tions. . . . All these subtle little inklings, carefully prudent and ortho-dox to the times, as indicated by my responses, clearly make *Vanity Fair* a Victorian novel.

Z. When I tabulated my general responses this was the breakdown: Amusement—Enjoyed Sarcasm: 14 times; Snicker: 4 times; "How true": 5 times. . . . [A] part which amused me was Thackeray's play on words [re: Becky and Lord Steyne] "He besought, he implored . . . his sister-in-law to be watchful in her intercourse with that noble-man." . . . I thoroughly enjoyed Thackeray's cynicism and sarcasm. . . . I think it was the "snickers" that I liked best, however, and a couple of times I grunted out loud. . . . My favorite snicker is where Sir Pitt Crawley is being described: ". . . Never advanced any senti-ment which was not perfectly trite and stale. . . ." Since *Vanity Fair* dealt with such topics as hypocrisy and social climbing, one could detach himself from the story and sit back and enjoy it. . . . I felt safe throughout the story. I think this is why it is a Victorian novel. . . . the novel deals with human faults and weaknesses, but doesn't call a spade a spade. This, I think, is Victorian.

A^2. The entire sarcastic tone . . . seems to derive from an inability or unwillingness of the author to deal with women on their own terms. . . . I'm attracted by the aloofness and disdain with which many British writers deliver their moral themes. I like the "author intrusions" for their very air of authority (even if it be hollow) and unspoken indifference for the reader. . . . [Amelia and Dobbin] would be generally "good" in our society for the same reasons they were in theirs—they're universals with no Ego, much less an Id.... complete lack of overt sexuality—a masterfully designed vehicle without a motive force. . . . very little gradation or sensitivity— no subtlety or tenderness. The complete lack of oversexuality is mysterious and amusing. . . . I like Rebecca. She is the main motive force in the novel, manipulating everyone around her. . . . I like the opulent life-style of *Vanity Fair* and, empty as its mores are, I'd be only too happy to try it . . . the emphasis is on subdued, passive action, and probably does contribute to the voyeuristic mood, even of the author. . . .

B^2. The general thing I noticed . . . was that it skipped over the love scenes . . . it seemed that there was something lacking throughout the novel: it was sex that I missed. . . . In the gaps in *Vanity Fair*, the action is always alluded to in one manner or another . . . Thackeray talks about when two unmarried persons get together, blah, blah, blah. . . . I felt like a starving man who is being tormented by someone dangling a piece of meat just out of reach . . . the . . . novel is saved, or was for me, by the fact that often something is more intriguing unsaid than said; what makes the neighbor's eyes bug out over the back fence is just as much the fact that something juicy happened as the thing itself does. . . . It was more or less like a game the reader played with the novel, Name the Sin. . . . This is what makes *Vanity Fair* so much better than some dime store piece of shit that not only gives the reader the coloring book, but colors it in.

C^2. I am able to grasp an image of Amelia as not so much being a prude and trying to sexually tease males with her face, but of not quite being aware that her face must somehow stand for the rest of her body . . . [Rebecca] . . . is fully conscious of her sexual attraction and uses it. . . . *Vanity Fair* . . . is presented as sort of a huge B-52 crammed with a very rigid set of rules for what one can or cannot do when one is "on the make." The feeling is that this huge B-52 took off some time in the distant past, loaded with regulations . . . an uncountable number of times [Rebecca's] breasts are described. She likes to adorn them, and therefore call attention to them. Although she loosely adheres to the custom of dress, she hard-presses it to the maximum in sexuality. . . . Once a member of the permissive out-group [Rebecca] is introduced to high society, the whole manner of face-standing-for-body might very well collapse. . . .

Finding a Community Consensus

In reading through these responses only once, one perceives any number of different "groups" of opinions. However, let me call your attention to one element which may cause you to suspect that I "loaded" the assignment, that is, the judgment made by many of the respondents of what constitutes the "Victorian" quality of this novel. In presenting the problem to the class, I asked that each person present his affective response and his perception of things that struck him and try to derive from this material an idea of what he thought was Victorian about this novel. I presented no preliminary discussion of Victorianism, but counted on what people thought it might be, based on previous knowledge or prejudice. Some people did not present such a judgment, perhaps because they were so uncertain of the term as not to refer to it altogether. I say that you might consider this a loaded question because, in some way, the term Victorian is commonly understood and will therefore produce expressions of common value. But this does not prejudice the question I am exploring now; rather, it makes the common values even clearer. Since we are observing commonly held ideas of Victorianism, their importance lies in their similarity to each other. My claim is that this similarity is due not to an objective similarity among all concepts of Victorianism, but to the similarity of values of this relatively homogeneous group of students. I suggest furthermore that a good way to broach the issue of community held values is precisely to attach a value to a piece of literature and examine the resulting responses.

There are six respondents, P, Q, R, T, Y, and Z, who give an explicit reason why they thought the novel was Victorian—slightly less than half the fourteen. Of these, two—P and Z—are different from the other four. Respondent P says that the author's intrusions make it Victorian, and Z says that his feeling of safety while reading is what does it. The other four deal with topics of womanhood, love, or sex. Z also says it is Victorian because the novel "doesn't call a spade a spade," and instead substitutes many fancy words. These words, in turn, are twice illustrated as the special work of the author. Thus, while P has a negative reaction and Z a positive one, they both find similar things to be Victorian. In the other four responses, we find a similar disjunction of values while speaking of the same topic: Q secretly envies Becky's sexuality, while R likens the book to making love "without ever achieving a climax." T and Y are more complex: T found the absence of sex "annoying" but enjoyed the value of "true love," while Y liked the suggestions of sexuality without its actual mention. Objectively, it would probably be possible to say that the four respondents "agreed" that some sort of sexual absence means that the book is "Victorian." If we put the two subgroups together we could say that according to these half-dozen readers, a Victorian novel is one with a strong intrusive author telling about unsexual women. According to my preconception of Victorianism, this sounds good. But the question remains, Do these responses really all add up to this?

If we look more carefully at responses Q and Y, for example, we note that they may well see sex in the novel, and Q admires Becky's aggressive breaking of rules. And if R did not really find any sex in this novel, why is her sexual imagery so vivid, saying that she was "suspended in a sexual climax"? Even P and Z are quite different from one another, in that the former is preoccupied with "the man that every girl dreams of marrying some day," while Z feels "safe" with indirect verbal usages. In terms of a definitive Victorian image, I don't think we can say they all picked out the same values *from the novel.*

However, if we view the responses as being produced by a group of adolescents about nineteen years of age, all the responses do in fact add up to an important preoccupation with sex and marriage, expressed in terms of the material presented in the reading experience. The respondents all picked out different material from the novel to demonstrate similar values. Our question is, In what sense are these values Victorian, and in what sense are they a reflection of the responding group?

It is perhaps important to note, before trying to draw conclusions about the values expressed by the responses, that these students have some understanding of what it means to write an emotional response. This can be seen, for example, in U's remark that the book "does a good job of suppressing emotional responses." They have all had some practice in speaking rather more freely in their work and in discerning the emotional lives of literary characters. However, the actual values they express are different enough from one another that there is very little possibility that the values were created by the act of lowering their inhibitions. This act, rather, simply allowed a freer self-expression.

To say that eleven of the fourteen respondents explicitly complain about the lack of overt sexuality in the novel and leave it at that would be to do an injustice to both the group of respondents and to the goal of our study. In no point of human development is sexuality the one and only factor, though it is never unimportant. It also won't do to say that these eleven are saying the same thing in different ways. More to the point would be to note that we here see a group of people of the same age, in the same culture, the same class, all expressing their individual versions of a universal concern. This concern is specific to our cultural community and to the specific stage of development the respondents are in. Consider the following group of remarks: R says, "'getting a booth at Vanity Fair' is no substitute for getting 'a piece of ass'"; V says, "there was not one good sex scene"; W complains about "the lack of swear words"; Y observes the "extreme prudence" with which the author handled the "obviously racy aspects of the characters' lives"; A² points out the "complete lack of overt sexuality"; B² says that the omitted love scenes made him feel like "a starving man who is being tormented by someone dangling a piece of meat just out of reach." I pick out such remarks to preface the question, What Victorian would respond to this novel in this way? What Victorian woman of nineteen would publicly speak of a "piece of ass"? And most generally, what Victorian would even see the novel as having omitted something? It can only be a contemporary—immediately contemporary— value that creates such a commentary. The prominence of films depicting sexuality, of novels and sex magazines released from censorship, all of which these students openly partake, could create such a widespread idea that sex is missing from this novel. In addition to the relaxation of classroom inhibition, there is the larger cultural relaxation which creates a certain level of sexual expectation in literature. These collective relaxations combine with the already strong subjective interest in sexuality to produce this observation about the novel.

This feature of the responses makes an important subsidiary point. It can be argued that a class will offer sexual responses if offered, say, *Lady Chatterley's Lover* to read. Then one can easily, though erroneously, argue that the content of the novel produced the content of the response. But when we find responses such as these to a novel like *Vanity Fair*, there is no way in the world of saying that prurient interest was evoked by the prurient material of the novel, and one can only ascribe the collective responses to shared personal and cultural values.

Clearly, there is much more to these responses than a large scale complaint about the absence of sexuality. There is a larger perception of how love is or should be handled. P says of Dobbin that he is "the type of sensitive yet strong man that every girl dreams of marrying some day." T says she does *not* find in the novel "the mutual sincerity I find so important in the 'true love' the Victorians looked for as much as I do." V finds sensuality in Becky in spite of the fact that there was "not one good sex scene" in the novel. X does declare that she believes "in the role of woman as wife and mother" and offers the proposition that "children, husbands, and a good life" are things that "most well-bred women" seek nowadays as well. And B[2], in spite of the fact that he is "starving," finds sensuality in the fact that "often something is more intriguing unsaid than said." These responses, and perhaps others that I did not cite explicitly, show that the concern with sexuality appears in an important complex of age-specific values—the hope of happy marriage, and the fun in being teased. It is interesting how R and X oppose T on the *same* issue: the personal ideal of "true love" is satisfied for the former two but not satisfied for the latter. Again this kind of discrepancy can be explained only by the supervening nature of subjective perception and not by some decision that one or the other valuę definitely does or does not appear in the novel.

A further variation of the themes of love and sex appears in responses R, S, and T. Respondent R observes that the author seems to her "very feminine." S finds, in part, an "effeminate" quality in "tableaus and character," while he describes Jos as the "fat feminine brother." Respondent T "did not enjoy the emasculization of men." In all of these responses, the feelings appear as part of a larger mood of social degeneracy students found in the novel, and which they felt, on the whole, was repulsive. In this theme also, one wonders how Victorian a value this is, since the prominence of homosexuality in our own culture is what creates the connection in students' minds between effeminacy and social degeneracy. On a personal level, adolescents are extremely sensitive to what it takes to create an unambiguous sexual identity. Again, these responses are better understood in terms of currently held group values than in something characteristically "Victorian."

Juxtaposed to this major idea of love, marriage, and sexuality, the responses show an equally strong attention to the role of the author-narrator, which is alluded to in twelve of the fourteen responses. In the world of professional criticism, it is not a matter of much debate that this particular characteristic of explicit comment by the author-narrator in fiction is commonly found in Victorian novels. It is, after all, a matter of fact and not of judgment. For readers such as these, who are not professional critics and who have read literature of other periods, it would be surprising if there were no perception of this prominent feature of the novel's style. The question for us to explore is exactly what value these readers place on this fact and what role this value plays in the overall drift of their responses.

The majority of those who mentioned the author show an extremely strong response. Respondent P "became very close to Mr. Thackeray and his novel." R says, "Thackeray *is Vanity Fair,* and if you don't like the author as a person, which I didn't, you simply can't like the book." S says, "Thackeray himself does not escape my mocking laughter" and "repeats his sermons on Sammyism . . . till I am about to puke." W says, "The author's intrusions formed a good part of the story and . . . [they] would amuse and amaze me." X says that Thackeray's "commentaries kept me from throwing the book down and giving the whole mess up to the wind." Respondent Z "thoroughly enjoyed Thackeray's cynicism and sarcasm," and A^2 liked Thackeray's intrusions "for their very air of authority (even if it be hollow) and unspoken indifference for the reader."

Except for overall judgments of whether the author's comments were enjoyable or not, there is no pattern of factual observation in these comments. Even R's judgment that Thackeray *is* the novel is not shared by the others I cited, and certainly not by the others I did not cite. However, can we find any element of adolescent psychology that might bring some of these remarks together? In the comments of P, R, S, and A^2, there is a strong sense of authority associated with the author. For P it is an emotional authority, as it is for R. For S and A^2 it is a social and religious authority, while for W and X, it is a psychological authority— the author is smart enough to anticipate one's own thoughts. Only for respondent Z is the author an entertainer. In a somewhat different context I discussed how typical it is for an adolescent to seek authority to emulate. You might like to point out that a strong authority figure is commonly found in Victorian culture, and therefore the respondents are only "seeing what is there." Perhaps. But if we remember that our basic question is the *value* placed on this authority, we see how much this value is a function of the individual reader. It is not particularly Victorian, for example, to become "close" to an author, or to like or dislike him "as a person." This is a universal feature of people's response to literature, from the very beginning when poetry was recited by a minstrel. In the intimacy of the reading situation, things especially Victorian are not of first importance, although the values can subsequently be conceived as Victorian. Therefore, the great attention paid to the author is explainable as a typically strong adolescent response to authority, a kind of "make or break" situation that R describes. For X, Thackeray saves the book, while S sees his comments as "sermons on Sammyism" which help develop nausea in him— a strong aversion to the religious tonality he sees. While A^2 is less extreme, he does come right out and say that he enjoys the air of authority for its own sake, that is, "even if it be hollow." Z is probably the most adult, for he detaches himself enough to laugh at the whole business and sort of laugh along with the author. Both Z and A² take pleasure in the author; they seem more relaxed and more accepting of authority since they are able to perceive it as tongue-in-cheek—not as serious or compelling.

Other responses to Thackeray help relate the author's intrusions to the concerns of love and sex we observed earlier by adding to the response to Thackeray yet a third thought. T says that she enjoys "his dialogue." U is "disturbed and impatient with Thackeray as he substituted words into the place of emotional reaction . . . and fearfully fails to carry through." Also, everyone but Becky is "carefully dressed up in mounds of flaccid verbiage." Y remarks on Thackeray's interjection that the very subject he raised "ought not be talked about in a book." And B² says that the novel "is saved" by the very fact that Thackeray does *not* talk about what happens when two unmarried people get together, because it is "more intriguing unsaid than said."

With this theme we return to where we began our discussion of literary importance—words, and the awareness of how words actually develop our reading experience. In the remarks that I have just cited, and perhaps in others you may observe yourself, the awareness of the novel's language has an important connection to the feelings about the author's authority and those about love, sex, and marriage. Consider, for example, the remarks of B². This respondent says that Thackeray "talks about" when two unmarried people get together. He then says that the important matters are "unsaid" and are "more intriguing" that way. This observation can mean only one thing (to this respondent), namely, that certain kinds of talk are substituted for certain kinds of other talk. Respondent U observes this very situation, but with a negative value: he is "disturbed and impatient" when Thackeray "substituted words into the place of emotional reaction." For respondent B² words seem to heighten the imaginative interest in sexuality, while for respondent U, they suppress or hide the object of interest. In both cases, the use of words is directly attributed to the author. Therefore, the author is viewed by these two readers as the person who is regulating their emotional interest in the reading experience. More particularly, even, it is through this response to words that we learn of the differing values each reader brings to the work. For the one, the words help reveal feeling; for the other they help conceal it. Subjectively, it is not the words themselves which either conceal or reveal, but the *author*. The respondents perceive their feelings as being regulated by an authoritative *person*: "If you don't like the author as a person, you can't like the novel."

The reading transaction is in fact conceived altogether as a relationship between the reader and his feelings, a relationship that is regulated by the author, who will either facilitate or prevent the reader from having a satisfactory experience. If you think about this situation, it is quite remarkable. The author is dead, and the reader is reading only because he wants to. Therefore, it can only be the case that the reader is creating this relationship as a result of an already established subjective orientation to his reading. This is the adolescent orientation about which we have been speaking. On the one hand, there is an intense spontaneous interest in sexuality; on the other there is an equally strong need for authoritative guidance in this interest. But reassurance, sanction, and justification are also sought from this authority, alongside the fear or suspicion that the interest will be denied or otherwise limited by authoritative intervention. In one or another of the responses, we observe every one of these factors at work.

Collective Subjectivity and Individual Truth-Value

Let us now consider the result of our understanding that both sexual interest and the need for authority are subjective. Two real and social factors now come into play in this connection. The first is the reality of the private and collective reading experiences in class; the second is the authority of the teacher. In this case, the task of the teacher is to use his authority to disclose what is commonly held in the community of readers—the class or the aggregate of responses. In the traditional classroom, this technique is used to show that the valid opinions of all members of the class are taken together to show what "is" Victorian about *Vanity Fair*. In other words, there is a gathering of perceptions and a generalization about the novel, the era, or something outside the classroom. In the subjective classroom, however, these matters can proceed only after the community understands its purpose with regard to itself.

We have already discussed how individual self-expression and self-awareness proceed before anything else. With regard to this group of responses to *Vanity Fair,* we have seen that the common features of the responses are traceable to the concerns of adolescence before anything else. We have seen that common features have to do with what values prevail in our own culture. Thus, the group of responses represents a kind of social subjectivity and suggests what I mean by "collective subjectivity." If, in the traditional method of getting a generalization from an aggregate of opinions, we were to ask the teacher how "true" he thinks that generalization is, he would say, "Why, we do in fact have a reasonably true picture of Victorian values, since we have so many different perceptions which entered into our conclusion." My question is, "True to what?" Is there really some way of testing the truth or falsity of the meaning of "Victorian"? Is there such a thing, as Q says, as a "Victorian Code for Women"? Are the "subtle inklings" that Y thinks to be typically Victorian definable in an absolute sense? Is, as Z says, feeling "safe" while reading the novel something that is easily recognized as a Victorian feeling? And so on. We learn now that even the attempt to say what is Victorian on the basis of a group of judgments is an objectification of what is happening in the collective subjectivity of the class. The fact emerges that a sense of what is meant by "Victorian" can only be defined as a reaction to unspoken, contemporary, collective, and subjective values. If you find this hard to believe, try to define for yourself "the American mind of 1975." You can immediately see how preposterous a task this is, since yours *is* the American mind of 1975, and you can't project your values onto something else, as you can do with the Victorian mind, which is, by definition, something that is not you.

There is no avoiding the subjective authority of the community of respondents. In the classroom, the teacher's authority is an effigy of the author's authority in the reading experience. However, the other members of the class comprise a social authority, a reminder of the values that the reader shares with others in his own group. Therefore, the fruit of a class studying its own responses in aggregate is an understanding of the values that are held by virtue of the group's existence in the first place. The decision about what is "true" about English Victorians is, before it is anything else, a decision of what is true of that group. The truth of the decision about what is Victorian is measured only by the breadth of agreement that decision can garner—only by the extent to which that decision reflects commonly held subjective values. If the decision is tested outside the classroom, it goes through a similar process: Does it reflect the collective subjectivity of the whole community of readers of *Vanity Fair*? Interpretation is always a group activity, since the individual interpreter is creating his statement in large part with an eye toward who is going to hear it. That is his community, whether it is of students, teachers, reviewers, or critics. It is a commonplace in criticism to say that what our age thinks is true of the Victorian is not necessarily what another age will think. The history of Shakespeare criticism clearly bears this out. But "ages" are not the only groups which exercise their subjective prerogatives in interpretations. The identical process takes place in the classroom. Just as an individual opinion is created to handle private feelings and associations, a group opinion is created primarily for the well-being of the group and not for the "truth" of the object of that opinion. For this reason interpretation is a communal act, serving the collective subjectivity rather than an external absolute standard of truth.

Instead of the standard of objective truth, we may now use the idea of *truth-value*. Consider C^2's rather contemporary image of a "huge B-52" which "took off some time in the distant past, loaded with regulations" as describing what Q called the "Victorian Code for Women." This "code," which I suggested was not explicitly definable, is in fact "definable" in terms of respondent C^2's image, which adds a sense of overwhelming power to the set of rules— for me. Each response-judgment has a certain truth-value for me, in the sense that I can assimilate them both and make them part of my feeling about my reading experience. Each member of a group creates "the truth" through his response to other responses. What appears true to us is, above all, characterized by our inward conviction of belief in a proposition, a conviction subsequently validated by the assent of other authorities—group or individual. In the classroom, I believe the most important thing to be done is to nurture the ability to develop convictions responsibly based on our tastes. If we are able to understand the subjective context in which convictions are developed—in which people finally decide on what is for them true or false in life—a whole new aspect of our personalities is released. Feelings—that part of us longest with us and most common in daily experience—are responsibly welcomed into public discussion. Our traditional sense of classroom or public reality is finally made to correspond with our subjective sense of private reality.

Using This Book:
Pragmatic Suggestions and Elaborations

It will occur to anyone who reads this book, especially someone experienced in the classroom, that while understanding an idea like "truth-value" is one thing, creating the circumstances for studying it in the classroom is something else. Classes and courses rarely fit exactly what we plan for them, and most often they develop a shape of their own, guided by the personalities of the students and by their interactions with the teacher. I can recall how in elementary school I listened with a great sense of mystery to teachers taking the trouble to characterize "this class"; for example, "this is the laziest class I have ever met." I wondered how, with thirty-five-odd students in the class, the whole class could be "the laziest." As I grew older and became a teacher, I began to understand that my childhood perception of the class was not erroneous but different. I had viewed "the class" from the standpoint of my own needs and expectations, and my teacher had viewed it from her own analogous standpoint.

Part of the aim of this book has been to demonstrate that literature exists altogether on the basis of the subjective re-creation of the reader. A classroom likewise exists as the subjective re-creation by the teacher and the members of the class. In using this book, therefore, it is especially important that teachers take the time and energy to understand who is in the class and to define its uniqueness in terms of its constituent individuals. While no amount of training can anticipate the characteristics of a class, an enlightened teacher can make the effort to tell himself how he feels about each individual. These feelings will be the varying factor deciding just how much emphasis should be placed on each part of the program of study I have outlined above.

As I have outlined them, the four steps of the program represent a logical and psychological sequence. This sequence may be followed exactly as I have outlined it, if the teacher wishes, since the main aim of each element in the sequence is labeled in its subtitle. However, there are alternative and additional ways of getting most of the main points across in class. In the following four short sections, I have suggested several lines of inquiry which might be of some guidance to both teacher and class in discussing the issues raised by this book. The questions themselves may be used in any way best suited to the taste of the class—in an oral discussion, as a journal assignment for subsequent discussion, as an essay assignment, as a student-led class forum—any context, really, that the class wishes.

Thoughts and Feelings

Each of the following lines of inquiry may be used to demonstrate one or more of the following points of this section: (1) showing how feelings exist here and now; (2) provoking the class; (3) affect; (4) associations and analogies; (5) analysis of anecdotal material; (6) participation of teacher and students in a common schedule of emotional development.

(a) Tell the class of a recent dream. What do others perceive about how the dreamer told his dream? How interested are others in hearing someone else's dream? What kinds of material does the teller use to explain his dream? In what way does a dream mean more to the dreamer than to others? How does the significance of the dream change from when one is dreaming to when one is telling the dream? Under what circumstances would you change a dream for a public telling? What kind of private experiences can't be discussed in public?

(b) Tell of a recent argument with a parent. Are the feelings you experienced in the argument unique to the argument, or are they present at other times and only "came out" in the argument? How do you perceive your parent in the argument? How do you think your parent sees you? Why is there a similarity between arguments you have with your parents and arguments other people your age have with theirs? What feelings are aroused in those who hear about the argument of one person with his parent? What influence do the feelings brought out in the argument have on other aspects of your life? How are feelings about parents connected with feelings about teachers? (Try to answer this question using a specific parent and a specific teacher.) Is school a place where you get away from arguments at home, where you overcome bad feelings about the argument, where you continue to have bad feelings, or what?

(c) Describe what you think is the most successful moment of your life. Try to reexpress this moment in terms of a few analogies —"this success was like peeling the skin from a suspended grape." Is it a success of private achievement or public accomplishment? What other people are associated with the feeling of success? Do you feel that anything was demonstrated to yourself or to others in this success? What aggressive or hostile feelings do you find in this moment of triumph? What fears, if any, can you associate with this feeling of success?

(d) Tell of a moment of great embarrassment or shame. Could this feeling have occurred if it had not been associated with other people? Can a feeling of embarrassment be associated with anyone, or are only certain people eligible to have participated in your feeling, or to have contributed to it? In order for you to feel shame, what kinds of events or experiences must have preceded it? When you did feel it, what was your immediate response? Does your immediate response help to tell you what caused it to begin with? Compare two embarrassing moments in your life, what preceded each, and what your responses were in both cases. Can you be embarrassed before yourself? What kinds of thoughts can you have that would embarrass you, even if no one else knew them?

(e) Try to recall the worst teacher you ever had. What are the specific attributes of this person that made you feel he was "the worst"? Describe how you feel with this teacher, alone and in class. Think of your response to the present teacher in comparison to the worst teacher. What considerations would regulate your criticisms of the present teacher? What ways are open to you to express negative responses to a teacher in class? What good do you think it might do for you? What kinds of feelings do you have about yourself when you find you have bad feelings about someone else? What are your expectations when you meet a new teacher? What is the "ideal" teacher? Has this ideal ever been fulfilled?

(f) Try to remember your earliest feeling of love. Was it directed toward a parent, an animal, a baby sibling, or a food or a toy? When you felt love, then, how would you describe your "loving" behavior? How would you describe your relationship with the loved object? How much did you have power or authority over what you loved, and how much did it have power over you? How much did you depend on what you loved, and how much did it depend on you? Do you love what you need or need what you love? What is the connection between how you loved as a child and how you love now?

Feelings about Literature

This section argues that the natural and familiar feelings of everyday life are the same ones which appear in one's response to literature. The three components of response— perception, affect, and association— represent an application of the basic principles of obtaining and studying response discussed in the first section. The procedures I outlined may be followed directly or may employ other poems or stories. It is also possible, however, to teach the material in this section without yet narrowing the context to literature. The following suggested lines of inquiry set forth several nonliterary contexts which nevertheless keep the general framework of studying response to *symbolic* objects.

(a) Try to remember the last time you cried in a movie. Describe the scene and the situation in as much detail as you can, as well as the reasons you thought you were so moved to tears. Do you feel it is strange to have a tangible physiological response to something imaginary? How might you account for this phenomenon? What do you think was the actual cause of your crying? What do you think is going on in your head when you observe a virtual, or symbolic, object? When you respond to a movie, is it working on you, you working on it, or you working on yourself? When you decide to watch a move, what, with regard to your own feelings, are you deciding to do?

(b) Describe a favorite doll, teddy, security blanket, or similar toy you had when you were a small child. What role did it play in your life? What things, besides itself, did it represent? In what kinds of situations did you find the toy a comfort? Of what benefit was it to you to have one toy stand for many things or people? Is there any single affect or feeling common to all the situations occupied by the toy? How many other people in your life at the time were involved with you in playing with this toy? Was it something you could or could not share, or didn't it matter? How did your relative willingness to share your toy reveal what you felt about it deep inside? In what respects might this toy be like a poem or other work of art?

(c) Think back to the last time you were at a sports event with a large cheering crowd. If you were rooting for a team, try to describe these "rooting" feelings in a particular situation. For example, what did you want a particular player to do at a particular time, and why? How would you account for the fact that you are capable of wanting a teenager to drop a ball into a hoop with the same intensity that you want to succeed in school or in love? What, beside athletic ability, do you take pleasure in at a sports event? Do you think an athletic team or star represents some part of your personality? Why do you suppose some people become hysterical at ball games? What is the nature of your concern for the outcome of a game in which you are not playing?

(d) Compare two different photographs of the same object, one a closeup. Is the "object" in both photos still "the same"? To what extent does it matter to know that you are looking at the same object? How does your response to the two pictures differ? Compare in some detail the different feelings you have looking at something close up versus looking at it from a distance. To what extent is the photo an "accurate" representation of the object, as opposed to the photographer's personal view of it? Is it possible to observe any object without the interference of the means you have of perceiving it? What do you suppose is meant by "reliable" perception?

(e) Pick an object or a person and, along with four or five others, draw it as fully as possible in five or ten minutes. To what extent, and in what ways, are the differences in the drawings not due to differences in drawing ability? Find out what each person thinks about why he drew the item the way he did. How does one distinguish between drawing ability and accuracy or sophistication of perception? What feelings or associations does each person have about, first, the object, and second, his drawing of the object? Is there any systematic relationship between the feelings about the object and those about the drawing? Can you tell by looking at the drawings alone what aspects of it are subjective representations by the artist? If an object is drawn almost exactly the way it looks to you, does this mean it is an "accurate" representation? Is it possible for an artist to draw something "exactly" the way "it looks"? Why or why not?

(f) Discuss or present a favorite item of clothing. What feelings do you have about this item, beyond your dependence on its functional utility? Detail the reasons why it is a favorite. How many of these reasons have to do with the actual use of the item? How many of the actual uses are in fact completely necessary? What purpose would you say such a favored item serves in your life? To what extent does clothing have to do with how you feel about yourself? To what extent does the item represent something other than itself? How do your feelings about this item relate to your general attitude toward clothing—your overall concern with the effect clothes have on your public appearance? To what extent is the value of this favored item associated with certain people in your life and how you feel with and about these people?

Deciding on Literary Importance

The question of literary importance is meant to raise the issue, "importance to whom"? There are three possible alternative answers to this question—to the story, the author, and the reader. At various points in the main discussion the implications of these alternative answers are considered. As with the previous sections, the sequence of study may be implemented as I outlined it, pursuant to my overall psychological rationale. The following sets of questions will give some idea of the dialectic that might help bring out in class the issues I have discussed. Again, their sequence or relative stress in actual usage may be altered to suit the teacher's own plans and tastes.

(a) Suppose you decide that X is the most important element in the story. What were your criteria for making that judgment? To what extent does your judgment depend on what you alone see in the story? What kinds of prejudices or predispositions did you *bring to* the story that might have led to this judgment? To what extent is your judgment a reflection of your personality, or a reflection of feelings you had while reading? What would you say is the difference between a feeling about the story and a judgment about it? In order to know how you feel, do you make a decision or a discovery? In making a judgment, is it a decision or a discovery?

(b) Write down the things in the story that especially strike your fancy; these can include a phrase, a character, an event, a scene, a usage, a mood, anything to which you can apply the phrase, "I like this." If you like something, is it important? Are you willing to say that something important to you is also important to the story or to the author? If something is important to you, what does this mean pragmatically, in terms of your behavior, responses, and feelings? Can something be important to the story that is not important to you? Describe a situation in which this is the case. Is there any difference between what *is* important in the story and what *you think* is important?

(c) Suppose you record all your feelings about the story—your affective and associative responses—and then you come to a judgment as to what was most important. How much does setting down your feelings affect the judgment you make? Can you then make a judgment independent of your feelings? Suppose you do not record your feelings—is your judgment then more independent of your feelings? Why or why not? Write down your feelings, your judgment, in that order, and then look them over. Do you see any connections between them? Do you see any systematic differences? What conclusions would you draw from either the similarities or differences between your feelings and your judgments?

(d) Find a standard critical interpretation of one of the stories under discussion. Observe the terms in which the interpretation is presented. How many of the judgments are opinions and how many are facts? If the interpretation is all facts, is it still an interpretation? Likewise, if it is only an opinion, is it still an interpretation? How much of what you consider guesswork is involved in the interpretation? How do you go about deciding how true, valid, or relevant the interpretation is? Is the truth of an interpretation the same as the truth of Newton's laws? If so, how so, if not, why not? Why does a story need to be interpreted at all? Why can't it just be read, and then have everyone tell what is in his mind after reading?

(e) For one of the stories, have your teacher give his own choices of what is most important, as well as his reasons and his feelings. Having seen how your teacher responds, does this make a difference in your own attitude and frame of mind when you then respond to the same story? Do you feel more limited or more relaxed? Describe the ways in which you feel either way. How authoritative do you feel your teacher is? How authoritative do you expect him to be? How authoritative do you want him to be? Do you have a private sense that your teacher's feelings are "righter" than yours? Or is the situation the reverse, where you think your feelings and reasonings are more authoritative, but you can't just come out and say so? How do you suppose hearing your teacher's feelings and reasons can teach you anything? What authority are you willing to let your teacher have over you?

(f) Think of yourself reading a story with a simple narrative format: an author telling about the doings of his hero, like "The Rocking-Horse Winner" and "Her First Ball." Do you feel you are listening to a report about the hero, or do you feel identified with the hero? Is there some point at which identification replaces your listener's attitude? If you are not identifying with the hero, in what sense are you "into" the story? If you feel at all times to be listening to a report, what makes you want to find out more about what is happening? What kind of feelings inside you make a story "interesting." Do you try to anticipate the end? What do you suppose is happening to you during reading that makes you want to find out the end?

(g) How conscious are you of the author's presence in the story?

To what extent do you wonder about his connection to the material of his story? Write down the things you are asking yourself about the author, questions that occurred to you during reading and afterward. Why do you suppose it is important for you to know about the author? Why should you have any response at all to someone you know almost entirely from the story he wrote? Do you find any connection between your response to the author—or your image of him—and your response to the story itself? Does it mean anything for you to know that there is an author out there *causing* you to respond? Is he in fact causing your response? If not, what is? Do you suppose the author had you or any other reader in mind when he wrote the story? Is there any way for you to tell what he wanted or intended a reader to feel? To what extent is your feeling of what is important in the story connected to what you think the author thought was important? Is your sense of importance determined by the author or by you?

(h) If the author meant to say something other than what it says in the story—that is, if he meant to give a "message"—why did he bother writing the story? Why not just give us the message? If he did not mean to say something else, what might have been the original purpose in writing the story? Why do you suppose you almost automatically think a story "means" something other than what it says?

(i) Is "meaning" something already "in" the story? If so, how would you point to it? Did the author put it there? If not, do you put it there? If you put it there, where did you get it? Did you find it in the story, or did you construct it out of your thoughts about the story? If you constructed it, what other ingredients went into your meaning aside from your thoughts about the story? Is it possible to avoid extra subjective ingredients in your meaning? To what extent does it seem like you *found* the meaning? Why does it seem so? What is the difference between finding a meaning and making one?

(j) Why does it seem strange to say that you "made" or constructed a meaning for a story? Will other people believe you more if you say you found it? Is your own credibility the only reason you prefer to say meaning is found? Or do you really believe that your meaning was found? If so, where did you find it?

Interpretation as a Communal Act

This section explores the question of how to make public use of knowledge derived from response and private reading experiences. Here again, there are various ways to pose this issue; for example, how does the teacher help create the interpretive views of the class, or how does each member of the class use the opinions of all the others. My own discussion tried to show that interpretive views of a group of similar people derive from group-subjective needs, and that an interpretation will aim to satisfy group needs as well as private ones. Here are a few lines of inquiry which might help a class to study some of the group functions of literary interpretation.

(a) If you read a story or a poem, and then tell no one about it, what effect does it have on you? Describe the various things that might happen in your mind before you tell anyone else about what you read. What different behaviors, feelings, or thoughts might you have if you tell someone about your experience? What does the act of telling others do to your sense of the original experience? What kinds of things happen during a conversation that affect your sense of the reading experience?

(b) Make the experiment of telling three or four different people, of differing age, sex, and relationship to you, about a story you read. Observe if and how *you change* what you have to say to each person. Record what you might expect each person to say to you. Is there anything for you to gain from such conversations? In real life, which people in your life would certainly hear from you about an interesting reading experience? Would you tell only people to whom you think the story is relevant?

(c) When you are in class, how much do you expect to learn from other students? Could you learn more from them or from the teacher? What effect might the opinions of unfamiliar peers (classmates) have on your own reading experiences? How many times have you read a book or seen a movie because others have and you want to be able to talk about it with them? If many people read books for this reason, what would you say is the function of books for them? Of what benefit is it to a small group of people to read the same book and talk about it?

(d) Observe the teacher give his own feelings and opinions about the story or poem under discussion. To what extent do you believe that other people's opinions and responses are affected by the teacher's? Do you perceive the class falling into groups for or against the teacher? Do most people pursue their opinions independently of the teacher's? When you are in a class discussion, do you feel you would somehow like to reach a conclusion that everyone should accept? If there is no exam on which you will have to write "answers," what kind of enlightenment could you expect from a class discussion of literature?

(e) To what extent do you use the occasion of a literary discussion to find out what other readers are like as people? To what extent do you look forward to hearing someone's response just because you know he is· an interesting person? Can a class be made to feel more like a group through a discussion of the same work of literature? If so, why should this be the case? When you are in a discussion, do you feel that "everybody else" is one group and you are another? Do you automatically perceive others' opinions as falling into a group? If so, why should this be the case? What would you say a classroom discussion about a story has in common with a dormitory bull session?

(f) Collect a series of written responses to a single work from your class and read them carefully. To what extent do you find yourself more interested in what the *readers* say than what they say about the *work*? How can you be mainly interested in the work and still aware of learning about other people and their common interests? To what extent can you separate a mutually agreed-upon interpretation from the needs and personalities of the agreeing parties? Except for the purpose of "learning something," what group needs do you think are met by public study of the group's responses?

Evaluation

In an ordinary context, evaluation means grading. In both school and university communities, the abuse heaped on grading is well known. Students and teachers alike find it a burden. Most new ideas in teaching try in some way to get around the need for a short significating evaluation. However, most administrators and those responsible for admissions to universities, graduate schools, and professional schools insist on the traditional grading system, if only to keep the admissions process easy to manage. If, suddenly, the admissions process were to become noncompetitive, the need for grading would vanish. But the need for evaluation would remain. Evaluation would take the form most suitable to the subject matter being taught.

The method of studying literary response proposed in this book is incompatible with traditional grading procedures. The response process is unique for each individual and will thus always be inhibited by the prospect of a coercive evaluation. That is, if a student is told that his grade in the whole course will suffer if he does not learn how to respond associatively, he will never be able to submit a response that will not somehow reflect the supervening influence of the threat. Since we are not dealing with questions of objective truth or falsity, but rather with questions of emotional and social viability, the authority of the teacher is experiential, not evaluative. One cannot set up a standard of response for the class to meet which will not, in application, result in the judgment of the student's character. A student will have real grounds to think he is a "C" person if his emotional responses receive that letter grade.

Evaluation of response capacity is already part of the response process. An individual already knows how deeply he is responding. If he has trouble knowing the depth of his response, this trouble must be analyzed without a coercive threat. If a student submits his response to public scrutiny, other respondents will be able to inform him of how sincere or participatory they think it is. Like expressions of love and affection, responses cannot be extracted from people; they must be evoked by the class atmosphere and by the work of literature under study.

I have discussed in some detail how one can tell whether a response is "useful" to both the respondent and to other readers. But each student must be himself persuaded of this usefulness before he can be expected to respond that way. This always takes time. Each person gets used to responding at a different rate. Some never feel at ease offering an associative response. These students, and others who are reluctant to respond in varying degrees, cannot be penalized. The fact of the matter is that these students may well have good reasons for their reluctance—personal reasons, or just an instinctive caution about the class or the teacher. If appropriate, such students can be attended privately, and the reluctance can be reduced by disclosing specific fears and inhibitions. Nevertheless, it must be anticipated that a substantial percentage of students will just not participate in the public submission of emotional responses. This means that not only will students be learning the response process at different rates, but that some will be doing different work altogether. In such a situation, uniform standards of grading are inadmissible.

Those doing "different" work are not excluded from learning the response process. This work is not really different at random. It is likely that those reluctant to write out emotional responses will be very ready to hand in "objective" analyses of the works they read. They will usually be eager to attack the literature from some traditional critical perspective, and they will enjoy developing theses and propositions about the work under study. I have already suggested, and in part shown, how this work can be utilized in the study of emotional response. Objectivist interpretive analyses can be examined for truth-value, and the originators of these analyses can be interrogated by the class to establish the assumptions of this kind of work. These assumptions may be publicly compared with the presuppositions of response-centered criticism (that is, the presuppositions of this book), and students may sort out on their own the intellectual advantages and problems in each orientation.

Inevitably, most of those wishing to try out the response method outlined above will be working within a traditional grading system. I assume that for those working in an unorthodox grading system— say, a full pass-fail curriculum—no special grading suggestions are in order. However, since this technique was developed over the past six or seven years in a traditional grading context, I would only want to pass on what has been a viable compromise between the evaluative methods demanded by the response process and the needs for a letter grade created by competitive admissions policies.

Two principles may be applied in determining a fair letter grade in a literary response course: (1) the amount of work produced by the student, and (2) the seriousness of purpose in the production of that work.

While part of the cynicism about academic life frequently comes from the fact that the longer paper sometimes gets the A, the sheer length of an associative response usually improves its viability. More associations and more details of feelings almost always bespeak a step closer by the respondent to the actual subjective complexity of his response. When inhibitions are reduced, and response is released, it is no longer a matter of churning out the required number of words to produce a substantial response. Associations and feelings just roll out, and it naturally becomes much more of a problem to curtail such responses to manageable length than to produce them to begin with.

Long and substantial responses cannot be produced by someone who is "lying" emotionally. That is, one cannot just write anything and expect it to be received as a genuine emotional response. Responses that seem superficial and trivial will usually be verified as such by the respondent, with the justification that he simply could not respond. On the other hand, if a student takes the trouble to fabricate a response—to produce associations that are not true or spontaneous—this is not an emotional lie, and the logic of these fabrications represents an emotional reality about the respondent. It is true that interpreting a fabricated response takes more dexterity than usual; perhaps it will involve further interrogation of the respondent. Nevertheless, it is emotionally germane that a response was fabricated because such use of the respondent's imagination represents a genuine emotional response to both the reading experience and the classroom situation. As a general rule, therefore, the length of the response is a fairly reliable index of the student's effort to participate in the response process.

No single response can be graded. Neither, as a rule, can one grade a group of responses. However, in applying the second principle of evaluation—the seriousness of purpose—the overall development of the response process in the individual is a key factor. Learning the response process means becoming more serious about oneself, and different people will develop this kind of seriousness at different rates. It could take until the last responses in the course for a student to become authentically involved; an overview of all his responses will point up the path to that involvement. Meanwhile, in open classroom discussions, attitudes are revealed that can be used to gauge the seriousness of the written response. For example, sometimes a defiant attitude in discussion is complemented by insincere responses; but other times, such an attitude is only a public defense for having exposed oneself in a full response. This is not so much a case of "classroom participation counts in determining your grade"; rather, oral discussion is an additional means of knowing the person's efforts at enlarging his responsive capacities. Thus, someone who says nothing in the open class may well be working just as hard as the habitual talker to explore his responses; in a response classroom silence is usually conspicuous and significant.

While the length and number of submitted responses is a relatively objective measure of involvement, the instructor's judgment of a student's overall effort is quite subjective. There is no way of denying or reducing this subjectivity. Furthermore, there is no final way of preventing abuse of this subjective exercise of authority. It is assumed that the vast majority of teachers have no reason to be maliciously capricious, and that their own seriousness of purpose will generate at least decency in the exercise of authority, and at most fairness and perspicacity. In addition, the grading procedure I am suggesting utilizes the teacher's subjective evaluation more in determining outstanding work than in judging failure or inadequacy.

My response courses have required a predetermined number of response essays of announced lengths. Those students who turn in all the essays—on time and in a cooperative spirit—receive a B in my course. If one or two essays are not turned in at all, or are turned in inconveniently late, the student's grade is reduced by a letter. Further delinquency results in further reduction of the grade. A grade of A can be achieved through outstanding work in a number of contexts. There might be, for example, a special fluency and eagerness in the production of associative responses. Such fluency usually bespeaks an important curiosity both about one's own responses and about the whole issue of emotional reaction to literature. On the other hand, a student may not be especially fluent in the production of responses, but may be able to handle analytically the interpretation of responses—his own and others. There is often a connection between a good analytical capacity and a relatively ordinary response-production ability: thus, while the responses of a good analyzer may be only adequate, he may be able to get exceptionally long mileage out of any given response. Another form of outstanding achievement may simply be in the skillful analysis of literature. Even though this is a response-criticism course, traditional literary analysis is especially useful in the class because it will provide examples of traditional literary judgment. The language of such judgments offers considerable insight into the mood in which such judgments are offered and provides clues to the emotional origins of the judgment.

The overall principle to be applied in awarding a grade of A is that any relevant form of excellence should be thus recognized. Any form of sustained and serious involvement in the work of the class must be rewarded. Excellence in the response process alone cannot be singled out as the only path to outstanding performance. This process is learned slowly, and all forms of literary interest contribute to it. The response-criticism classroom functions on a wider and more general conception of the literary experience than the traditional interpretive classroom. A teacher must be able to exercise more imagination and intellectual flexibility in establishing what excellence is. He should be able to work into the response discussion different kinds of literary response, different kinds of interpretive judgment, and different styles of judging literary importance. One of the illuminations disclosed by the study of emotional response is the multifarious styles, interests, and motives that each reader brings to bear on his reading experience. If a student can perceive any of these factors in his own experience, if he can establish for himself something really new to him about his own mental processes in reading, he can well be said to have achieved "excellence" in the study of literary response.

Grading in a response-criticism course boils down to a decision between what is adequate and what is excellent. This is no longer a quantitative decision, marked by the proliferation of incomprehensible distinctions between pluses and minuses. It is a qualitative decision that is, nevertheless, easily justifiable to the student in the great majority of cases. The process of evaluation, on the other hand, remains the complex and variable process that most people intuitively perceive it to be. It remains governed by negotiable judgments, by argumentation, and by interpersonal dialectic. Evaluation remains a function of both students and teachers rather than a didactic or authoritarian edict. In this way, this crucial process is given a new sweep and versatility, while the technical necessity of rendering a grade retains just those small dimensions of technicality and administrative necessity.

Short Bibliographical Guide to Study in Literary Response

In spite of the brevity of this book, and in spite of its lack of references to other works, the idea of literary response is extremely old and dates back at least to Aristotle, who defined tragedy in terms of the emotional response to it: pity and fear. He also conceived literature as cathartic for the audience—literature is a stimulus for emotional purgation. This view of literature has long exercised an influence on literary thinkers. However, it was not elevated to the status of a system of literary thought until Freud began including literary experience as part of the data in his systematic conception of human psychology. Freud adopted Aristotle's view of literature—and he implicitly adopted Aristotle's judgment of the greatness and importance of Sophocles's play Oedipus Rex—and he used the popularity of both Hamlet and Oedipus Rex as the fundamental criterion of their cultural interest. Because of Freud's work, it became possible to view Samuel Johnson's criterion of good literature—that which "pleases many and pleases long"—as part of a larger and more organized conceptual system which gives the audience a major role in establishing the value, the meaning, even the existence of a work of literature. This system also includes Coleridge's famous insight that literature does not really function until the audience "willingly suspends disbelief." In general, a great many time-honored insights and intuitions about the key role of literary response in human culture were tied together by the new understanding of literary experience as a species of overall psychological functioning.

It is obviously impossible to review here the major documents in the history of criticism to isolate the idea of literary response. It is possible to show, however, what has been the history of empirical response studies in the last five decades or so, and to indicate how this work emerges from this historical development. We may say that the idea of studying the actual responses of actual readers is quite modern, and that it began under the influence of a synthesis of old insight into literature and new insight into human psychology.

The first important modern study of literary response was I. A. Richards's *Practical Criticism* (1929; now available in paperback from Harcourt Brace Jovanovich). Richards brought together a group of respondents' readings of eight different poems and showed how almost every reader misread the words of the poems under the influence of his prejudices and carelessness. The prevailing thesis of the book is that a great many personal and subjective factors stand in the way of responsible objective reading. However, in an important way, Richards stood in two intellectual camps. One camp was New-Critical: that is, he believed in the fundamental purpose of learning to read literature faithfully because he believed in the enduring integrity and autonomy of the work of art. The other camp was much more psychological, and in his earlier work, *Principles of Literary Criticism* (1925, now also in paperback from Harcourt Brace Jovanovich), Richards went to great lengths to describe and demonstrate the subjectivity of aesthetic value judgments. He believed in the necessity of developing a psychology of literary judgment. Thus, while recognizing for the first time that real readers' responses must be studied in order to develop such a psychology, Richards implied that such a psychology is normative, and that different responses and different readings can be "corrected" on the basis of that norm.

The idea of normative readings prevailed for about three decades after Richards, owing to the prestige and academic workability of the New Criticism. During that time it became increasingly clear that the rigorous study of literary response is incompatible with the idea of normative readings. Part of the evidence for this incompatibility was that even in the presentation of New-Critical normative readings in professional journals there was (and is) continuing disagreement with regard to what constitutes a "correct" reading of any given work. Because of the continued adherence to normative readings alongside the proliferation of contradictions to this idea, it fell to the lot of a kind of fringe group —the psychoanalytic critics—to explore the question of literary response. Unfortunately, however, even among these critics the standard of normative readings prevailed, and with even more intensity, since many psychoanalytic critics believed that their analyses reached a kind of rock bottom answer to all problems of literary interpretation. It is as if normative readings were the defining idea of all literary enterprise, no matter what the orientation of the critic.

Gradually, within the group of psychoanalytic critics, the contradiction between normative readings and the manifest variability of reader response led to more searching inquiries into the psychology of reading and of literary judgment. The first important study of this kind was Simon O. Lesser's *Fiction and the Unconscious* (Boston: Beacon Press, 1957; now out of print). This book was fundamental and comprehensive in that it posed the pragmatic and empirical questions that we are exploring today. Lesser discussed at length the motives for reading, the psychological orientation of the reader, the appeal of certain enduring features of all literature, and the actual state of mind of the respondent. Through his discussion of "analogizing" (the conscious and unconscious analogies the reader creates in response to what he reads) Lesser suggested a rational framework for the understanding of multiple readings of the same work. Although Lesser did not analyze actual reader responses, his conception of the reader's mind and motives made it possible for the systematic study of reader response to proceed.

Before I discuss the work that pursues Lesser's thinking most rigorously, let me note parenthetically two rather recent works which explore the increasing present-day need for dealing with multiple interpretations. They are Walter J. Slatoff's *With Respect to Readers* (Ithaca: Cornell University Press, 1970) and Richard L. McGuire's *Passionate Attention* (New York: W. W. Norton & Co., 1973). Neither of these works has a theoretical orientation; rather, they are exhortative works asking the reader to learn of and use different ways of thinking about literature. I would describe their presentational style as "conversational," and in this regard somewhat annoying because of the pervasive implication that literary experience is ineffable. In some sense, all emotional experience is ineffable; but this ineffability vanishes when a reader seeks either to share his experience by articulating it to others or to understand his experience by articulating it to himself. Once an experience is subject to articulation, it loses its intractable quality and becomes susceptible to systematic comprehension. Language is the means through which we provide ourselves with an emotional orientation in life. Therefore, articulated literary response may be even better understood not by applying several possible "theories," but by developing the most comprehensive and persuasive point of view of how human personality functions.

Toward this end, Norman N. Holland has done the most work to date in following through on Lesser's original suggestions. In a 1962 essay, "Shakespearean Tragedy and the Three Ways of Psychoanalytic Criticism" (*Hudson Review* 15:2 [Summer 1962]), Holland outlined how psychology has been applied to three dif-

ferent minds associated with literature: the author's, a character's, and the reader's. He pointed out that a character's mind does
not really exist, so we cannot study it; that the author's mind is
usually gone and biographical material scarce, and so it is difficult
to study it; but the reader's mind, our own, is alive and functioning, so that studying the reader's response is the most productive means of understanding the literary transaction. Following
this thinking Holland developed a theoretical model of literary
response in *The Dynamics of Literary Response* (New York: Ox-
ford University Press, 1968). This model reformulates many of
Lesser's suggestions, notably the fundamental act of the willing
suspension of disbelief, the defensive function of literary form,
and the automatic analogizing response that all readers bring to
their reading experience. While in this work Holland did not make
it clear how much he thought the reader develops "meaning" for
the work and how much he thought the meaning is already in the
work and only found by the reader, the main drift of his work was
to pay attention to what is going on in the reader's mind during
and after a reading experience.

In his most recent work, *Poems in Persons* (New York: W. W.
Norton & Co., 1973), and in *Five Readers Reading* (New Haven:
Yale University Press, forthcoming), Holland examines actual
responses of actual readers in depth, and in the light of his earlier
theoretical formulations. These works are closest to my own point
of view in this book and provide many response-analyses which
illuminate the response process. Detailed examination of real
responses has brought Holland, as it had similarly brought me, to
abandon the New-Critical presupposition of a work of art's inde-
pendence, and instead to view the work of art altogether in terms
of the reader's subjective re-creation of it. I know that this conclusion will be unacceptable to many readers and students of literature, but I believe it is inescapable once one has taken the trouble
to study literary perception and response with some rigor.

The reader is invited to carry the conclusions of response-
criticism in whatever directions he finds most compelling. It is
obvious that a great deal more needs to be understood about how
people function when they confront manifestations of language.
Language remains one of the most excruciating riddles of human
behavior. The multiplicity of languages invented by readers just
to say what they read and to tell how they feel about it, not to
mention the many "languages" (styles) already invented by writers
great and small, is testimony enough as to what needs to be
studied. This is a very large problem indeed, and it takes us into
the "bibliographies" of many disciplines hitherto only tangentially

relevant to "English"—philosophy, psychology, linguistics, aesthetics, child development, pedagogy, just to name some. Most of the works mentioned above have their own bibliographies and guides to further reading. I think that the reader interested in pursuing study in literary response will find enough questions in his own classroom to occupy a lifetime.